Moment mal!

A German Course
Glossary German-English 2

Vocabulary: Paul Rusch
Translation: Jerry Roth

Langenscheidt

Berlin · Munich · Vienna · Zurich · New York

The spelling in **Moment Mal!** corresponds to the Orthography Reform of 1996.

© 1998 Langenscheidt KG, Berlin and Munich

Printed in Germany · ISBN 3-468-47780-5

1 2 3 4 5 · 2002 2001 2000 99 98

Notes on the Use of the Glossary

1. Contents and Structure

The glossary contains words and phrases from Textbook 2 along with their English translations.

The glossary is arranged according to chapters and chapter sections of the textbook and contains all the words in the order of their first appearance. New words from the chapter headings are listed, where necessary, at the beginning of each chapter. Within the individual sections (A1, A2 etc.) phrases and keywords are listed in the following order:

First the words from the instructions in the margin; then the words in the main texts; and, finally, those in the corresponding sections (A1 etc.) of the blue conversation boxes at the bottom of the page. Individual keywords in bold face are given with the meanings they have in the respective context. Usage examples and idiomatic phrases appear in normal print.

2. Special Notes

2.1 Nouns

Nouns are given in the nominative, with the definite article and the plural. If no plural is given, this means that there is either no plural in German or that, if a plural does exist, it is used only rarely, or not in the context in question.

Nouns which occur only in the plural, either generally or in the contexts in question, are marked by (Pl.), e.g.:
die **Schulden** (Pl.)

For the formation of plurals, please refer also to Chapter 4, p. 29, of Textbook 1.

2.2 Verbs

Verbs are generally given in the infinitive. You will find a survey of the principle parts of irregular verbs in the appendix to the textbook.

2.3 Adjectives

Adjectives are listed in the basic uninflected form in which they appear after the verb "sein" (to be), e.g.:
wahr (basic form)
die wahre Welt (inflected form)

Indefinite pronouns and adjectives which are not used in their basic form but only with an ending are marked with a hyphen at the end, e.g.:
ober-
im oberen Stockwerk des Hauses

2.4 Stress

The main stress is indicated for every German word: _ indicates a long vowel or diphthong, . a short vowel, e.g.:
die **Stimmung**
die **Liebe**

2.5 How Certain Expressions Are Used

Regional and group-specific expressions are followed by explanations in parentheses. Colloquialisms and expressions current among young people are marked by an asterisk, e.g.:
die **Kohle** (*Umgangssprache: Geld)
das **Meteo** (schweiz. = Wetterbericht)

1 Hat man mit 17 noch Träume?

A1

die **Stimmung**, Stimmungen	mood
die Stimmung der Leute	mood of the people
zu	to (here in the sense of for/accompanying)
die Bilder zu Aufgabe 1	the pictures accompanying Exercise 1
locker	relaxed, informal
nachdenklich	thoughtful, contemplative
locker oder nachdenklich aussehen	to look relaxed or contemplative
selbstbewusst	self-assured, self-confident
sich selbstbewusst fühlen	to feel self-confident
wütend	enraged, furious
unzufrieden	dissatisfied
wütend oder unzufrieden sein	to be enraged or dissatisfied
protestieren	to protest
Jugendliche protestieren gegen die Welt der Eltern.	Young people protest against the world of their parents.

A2

wiedergeben	to report, to describe
interpretieren	to interpret
Aussagen wiedergeben und interpretieren	to report and interpret statements
der **Schlager**, Schlager	hit song, popular song
der **Schlagertext**, Schlagertexte	popular song lyrics
einverstanden sein	to be in agreement
Sind Sie einverstanden?	Is that all right with you?
weiterschreiben	to keep writing
der **Himmel**	heaven
die **Liebe**	love
der Himmel der Liebe	the heaven of love
nehmen	to take
etwas schwer (= ernst) **nehmen**	to take something seriously
Nimm das alles nicht so schwer.	Don't take all that so seriously.
stets	always
daran	of this/that/it etc.
stets daran denken	to always think of this/that/it etc.
der **Liebling**	loved one, darling
Liebling, das kannst du nicht.	Darling, you can't do/be that.

A3

auffallen	to stand out, to be noticeable, to strike
Was fällt Ihnen an der Sprache auf?	What strikes you about the language?
Techno	techno music
Berlin liegt im Techno-Rhythmus.	Berlin is pulsing with techno rhythm.
Love Parade (engl.)	Love Parade
Rund 600 000 Jugendliche treffen sich zur „Love Parade".	About 600,000 young people gather for the "Love Parade."
Neon-Gelb	neon-yellow
leuchtend	glowing, bright
Neon-Gelb und leuchtendes Orange	neon-yellow and bright orange
irr	crazy, insane, wild
pink (engl.)	pink
irres Pink	crazy pink
wahnsinnig	crazy, insane, wild
mint-grün	mint-green
wahnsinniges Mintgrün	wild mint-green
hin	there
bis hin zu	(all the way) up to
silbern	silver
alle Farben bis hin zu Enterprise-Silber	all colors up to Starship-Enterprise silver
bringen	to bring
das **Stadtbild**	city profile, cityscape
Farbe ins Stadtbild bringen	to bring color into the cityscape
das **Watt**, Watt (= W)	watt
die **Anlage**, Anlagen	system, equipment
die **Musikanlage**, -anlagen	electrical music-equipment
zahllos	innumerable
der **Fan**, Fans (engl.)	fan
Zahllose Techno-Fans tanzen auf der Straße.	Innumerable Techno-fans dance in the streets.
gedrängt	crowded
dicht gedrängt	crowded close together
der **Wahnsinn**	insanity
ein Riesen-Wahnsinns-Spaß	an absolutely incredible load of fun
Fun (engl.)	fun
Love (engl.)	love
Peace (engl.)	peace
echt	genuine, real
geil (* Jugendsprache: toll, großartig)	great, super
Fun, Love und Peace in einer echt geilen Stadt.	Fun, love, and peace in a really super town.

durchtanzen	to dance away
Ich will die ganze Nacht durchtanzen.	I want to dance the night away.

2 Jung und Alt

A4

die **Stellung**	position, opinion
Stellung nehmen	to express one's opinion
der **Song**, Songs	song
wahr	real, true
die wahre Welt zerstören	to destroy the true world
jagen	to hunt
treiben	to drive, to compel
lügen	to lie
betrügen	to deceive
reich	rich
das **Gesetz**, Gesetze	law
Reich und schön ist das neue Gesetz.	The new law says: Be rich and beautiful.
drehen, sich	to revolve around
die **Kohle** (* Umgangssprache: Geld)	money
Alles dreht sich nur ums Geld.	Everything revolves around money.
etwas selbst in die Hand nehmen	to take something into one's own hands
hergeben	to hand over, to give away
mehr	more, again
Nie wieder, nie mehr!	Never again, not any more!
der **Unterschied**, Unterschiede	difference
Welche Unterschiede gibt es?	What differences are there?

A5

formulieren	to formulate
Meinungen formulieren	to formulate opinions
der/die **Erwachsene**, die Erwachsenen	adult
Was denkt Lara über Erwachsene?	What does Lara think about adults?
das **Erwachsenwerden**	growing up, becoming an adult
naja . . .	well . . .
die **Freiheit**, Freiheiten	freedom
die **Schulden** (Pl.)	debts
fest	steady, permanent
die **Stelle**, Stellen	job
eine feste Stelle haben	to have a permanent/ steady job
langweilig	boring
der **Kompromiss**, Kompromisse	compromise
Kompromisse schließen	to make compromises

die **Mutter**, Mütter	mother
die **Erfahrung**, Erfahrungen	experience
erleben	to experience
ganz schön	quite, really
Das kann ganz schön unter Stress setzen.	That can really put you under stress.

A6

das **Heimatland**, -länder	native country
Wie erleben Sie Jung und Alt in Ihrem Heimatland?	How do you experience young and old in your country?

3 Moden früher und heute

die **Mode**, Moden	fashion, trend

A7

die **Beatles** (Pl.)	the Beatles
der **Rock**, Röcke	skirt
der **Minirock**, -röcke	miniskirt
der **Stichpunkt**, -punkte	keyword, main point
das **Erlebnis**, Erlebnisse	experience

A8

1965

dies-	this
in diesem Jahr	this year
das **Aussehen**	appearance
die **Generation**, Generationen	generation
eine ganze Generation verändern	to change an entire generation
männlich	male
das **Vorbild**, Vorbilder	model, example
nach Beatles-Vorbild	following the Beatles' example
wachsen	to grow
sich die Haare lang wachsen lassen	to let one's hair grow long
begeistert	enthusiastic
weiblich	female
begeisterte weibliche Fans	enthusiastic female fans
die **Ohnmacht**	faint
in Ohnmacht fallen	to faint
beeinflussen	to influence
die **Jugend**	youth, young people
die **Konvention**, Konventionen	convention
schaffen, sich	to create for oneself
Die Jugend schafft sich neue Konventionen.	Young people create their own new conventions.

1970

schockieren	to shock
Flower Power (engl.)	flower power
das **Haschisch**	hashish

die **Demonstration**, Demonstrationen	demonstration
die **Atomkraft**	nuclear energy
Vietnam	Vietnam
der Vietnam-Krieg	the Vietnam War
die **Sehnsucht**	longing
die Sehnsucht nach Liebe	longing for love
die **Gewalt**	force, violence
eine Welt ohne Gewalt	a world without violence
das **Motto**	motto
die **Hose**, Hosen	trousers, pants
die **Schlag-Hosen** (Pl.)	bell-bottoms
der **Pullover**, Pullover	pullover, sweater
der **Rollkragenpullover**, -pullover (= der Rolli, Rollis)	turtleneck sweater
der **Schuh**, Schuhe	shoe
dick	thick
der **Absatz**, Absätze	heel
„in" sein (engl.)	to be "in"
Schuhe mit hohen, dicken Absätzen sind „in".	Shoes with high, thick heels are "in."
der **Gitarrist**, Gitarristen	guitarist
der **Rock-Gitarrist**	rock guitarist
die **Dosis**	dose
die **Überdosis**	overdose
die **Droge**, Drogen	drug
Er stirbt nach einer Überdosis Drogen.	He dies after a drug overdose.

1997

der **Trend**, Trends (engl.)	trend
„Multi"	"multi"
Der wichtigste Trend heißt „Multi".	The most important trend is called "multi."
asiatisch	Asian
das **Kleid**, Kleider	dress
afrikanisch	African
die **Frisur**, Frisuren	hairstyle
erlaubt	allowed
Alles ist erlaubt.	Everything is allowed; anything goes.
zusammengebunden	tied together, tied back
super-	super-
superkurz	super-short
das **Hemd**, Hemden	shirt
die **Krawatte**, Krawatten	tie
die **Jacke**, Jacken	jacket
das **Arbeitsleben**	working life
hart	hard
Das Arbeitsleben ist hart genug.	Working life is hard enough.
Hip-Hop	hip hop
das **Schlagwort**, Schlagworte	catchword, catchphrase
die **Szene**	scene
die **Musik-Szene**	music scene
die **Esoterik**	New Age
boomen	to boom
das **Engagement**	involvement
dagegen	on the other hand, by contrast
die **meisten**	most people
„out" sein (engl.)	to be "out"
Die Esoterik boomt, politisches und soziales Engagement dagegen sind für die meisten „out".	New Age is "booming"; by contrast, for most people political and social involvement is "out."

A9

die **Diskussion**, Diskussionen	discussion
die **Fernsehdiskussion**, -diskussionen	television panel-discussion
halten von	to have an opinion, to think about
Was halten Sie von Mode?	What do you think about fashion?
modisch	fashionable
die **Kleidung**	clothing
Ich trage gerne modische Kleidung.	I like to wear fashionable clothing.

4 Kleider machen Leute

Kleider machen Leute.	Clothes make the man.

A10

das **Einkaufsgespräch**, -gespräche	conversation while shopping
führen	to conduct, to have
ein Einkaufsgespräch führen	to have a conversation while shopping
gucken	to (take a) look
Guck mal!	Take a look at that!
stehen	to look good on
Meinst du, der Rock steht mir?	Do you think the skirt looks good on me?
das **T-Shirt**, T-Shirts	T-shirt
das **Recht**, Rechte	right
Recht haben	to be right
brav	good, tame
Dieser Rock ist mir zu brav.	This skirt is too tame for me.
die **Einkaufsszene**, -szenen	shopping scene
Kann ich Ihnen helfen?	Can I help you?
das **Schaufenster**, Schaufenster	display window
anprobieren	to try on
das Kleid aus dem Schaufenster anprobieren	to try on the dress from the display window
meinen	to mean

Welches Kleid meinen Sie? — Which dress do you mean?

die **Größe**, Größen	size
Welche Größe brauchen Sie?	What size do you need?
probieren	to try (out/on)
Wo kann ich den Pullover probieren?	Where can I try on the pullover?
die **Jeans**, Jeans (engl.)	jeans
das **Sonderangebot**, -angebote	special offer
hübsch	cute
der **Fall**, Fälle	case, situation
Auf jeden Fall!	Absolutely!
umsehen, sich	to have a look around
Ich möchte mich nur umsehen.	I'd just like to have a look around.

5 Aussprache

A12
hoffentlich	hopefully
die **Melodie**, Melodien	melody

A13
der **Kern**, Kerne	core
der Kern der Information	the core of the information

A15
schwach	weak
„r" wird als schwaches „a" gesprochen.	„r" is pronounced like a weak "a."
die **Vorsilbe**, Vorsilben	prefix, syllable placed before a word or word stem
verlassen	abandoned, lonely, forlorn
vier Musiker, sehr verlassen	four musicians, very forlorn
drinnen	inside

6 Wortschatz

A16
die **Partikel**, Partikeln	particle
die **Dialog-Partikel**, -Partikeln	dialog particle

A17
die **Kiste**, Kisten	box
die **Wort-Kiste**, -Kisten	wordbox
Mensch!	Man!
Mensch, die ist super!	Man, that one is great!
schick	chic
gut	good
schön	good, nice
Gut und schön, aber . . .	That's all very well, but . . .
die **Zustimmung**	agreement
der **Zweifel**, Zweifel	doubt

der **Widerspruch**, Widersprüche	contradiction
die **Ablehnung**	rejection

A19
dabei	while doing so
Zeigen Sie dabei auf die Bilder.	Point to the pictures while doing so.
farbig	colored
die **Unterwäsche**	underwear
die **Unterhose**, -hosen	undershorts
der **Slip**, Slips (engl.)	panties
der **BH**, Bhs (= Büstenhalter)	bra
gemustert	patterned
gestreift	striped
die **Bluse**, Blusen	blouse
der **Anzug**, Anzüge	suit
der/das **Sakko**, Sakkos	jacket, sportcoat
das **Hemd**, Hemden	shirt
die **Brille**, Brillen	glasses
die **Sandale**, Sandalen	sandal
das **Paar**, Paare	pair
ein Paar Schuhe	a pair of shoes
leicht	light
der **Turnschuh**, -schuhe	gym shoe
die leichten Turnschuhe	light gym shoe
der **Stiefel**, Stiefel	boot
das **Unterhemd**, -hemden	undershirt
die **Badehose**, -hosen	bathing trunks
lässig	very casual, very relaxed
der **Badeanzug**, -anzüge	bathing suit
cool (engl., *Jugendsprache: überlegen; toll)	cool, great
die **Sonnenbrille**, -brillen	sunglasses
eine coole Sonnenbrille	a cool pair of sunglasses
der **Bikini**, Bikinis	bikini
die **Socken** (Pl.)	socks
die **Strümpfe** (Pl.)	stockings
der **Gürtel**, Gürtel	belt
das **Kostüm**, Kostüme	suit (for women)
der **Handschuh**, Handschuhe	glove
das **Sweatshirt**, -shirts (engl.)	sweatshirt
die **Mütze**, Mützen	cap
der **Schal**, Schals	scarf, muffler
dünn	thin
das **Tuch**, Tücher	cloth, scarf
ein dünnes Tuch	a thin scarf

A20
betrachten	to look at, to regard

A21
der **Koffer**, Koffer	suitcase
packen	to pack
das **Kofferpacken**	packing the suitcase

einpacken	to pack (into the suitcase)	der **Konnektor**,	coordinator
dazupacken	to pack (in addition, along with the other things)	Konnektoren	
		der **Satzteil**,	sentence part
		Satzteile	
		die **Definitionsfrage**,	*wh*-question (for more specific information)

7 Grammatik

		Definitionsfragen	
die **Textreferenz**	text reference, information	die **Marke**,	brand
die **Satzverbindung**,	compound sentence	Marken	
Satzverbindungen			

17 Lebensträume

der **Lebenstraum**, -träume	dreams and wishes for one's life

1 Traumgeschichten

die **Traumgeschichte**, -geschichten	story of a dream	**beugen**, sich	to bend down
		Sabine beugt sich zum Bruder.	Sabine bends down to her brother.
		flüstern	to whisper
		darauf	afterward
		gleich darauf	right afterward

A1

vorhaben	to intend		
der **Vordergrund**	foreground		
Im Vordergrund sieht man ...	In the foreground you see ...		
stürzen, sich	to throw oneself		
Der Mann stürzt sich von der Mauer.	The man throws himself down from the wall.		
annehmen	to assume		
Ich nehme an, dass ...	I assume that ...		
seltsam	strange		
Aber das ist seltsam.	But that is strange.		
unmöglich	impossible		

A4

der **Wunsch**, Wünsche	wish
davonfliegen	to fly off/away
Ich habe den Wunsch davonzufliegen.	I have the wish to fly away.
wegfliegen	to fly away

A2

erfinden	to invent, to make up
eine Geschichte erfinden	to make up a story
weitergehen	to continue
Wie geht die Geschichte weiter?	How does the story continue?
die **Idee**, Ideen	idea
Mama	Mama
Papa	Papa
der **Wagen**, Wagen/ Wägen	car
Papa wäscht den Wagen.	Papa is washing the car.
die **Ruhe**	rest, peace
in Ruhe lassen	to leave in peace, to stop bothering
der **Scherz**, Scherze	joke
Lasst mich in Ruhe mit euren Scherzen.	Stop bothering me with your jokes.
zu ... haben	to have to do
Ich habe noch zu tun.	I still have things to do.
die **Wahrheit**	truth
herunterkommen	to come down

2 Träume und Wünsche

A5

pflücken	to pluck
der **Traum-Baum**	dream tree
Pflücken Sie drei Blätter vom Traum-Baum.	Pluck three leaves from the dream tree.
das **Traum-Blatt**, -Blätter	dream leaf
die **Fantasie**	imagination, fantasy
die **Fantasie-Reise**, -Reisen	fantasy journey
der **Frieden**	peace
die **Sicherheit**	security
erfahren	to experience
Liebe erfahren	to experience love
das **Ansehen**	respect, esteem
gewinnen	to win, to gain
Ansehen gewinnen	to gain esteem
der **Erfolg**, Erfolge	success
verdienen	to earn
viel Geld verdienen	to earn a lot of money
glücklich	happy
der **Planet**, Planeten	planet
spazieren gehen	to (go for a) walk
Es war schön, dort spazieren zu gehen.	It was wonderful to go for a walk there.
weiterfliegen	to fly on/farther

A6

dav̱on	of
Ich träume davon wegzu-	I dream of flying away.
fliegen.	

3 Traum und Wirklichkeit

die **Wirklichkeit**	reality
Traum und Wirklichkeit	dream and reality

A7

die **Ausbildung**,	vocational training or
Ausbildungen	education
herumreisen	to travel around
verlaufen	to progress, to take its
	course
Ihr Leben ist ganz normal	Her life took a completely
verlaufen.	normal course.
die **Industriekauffrau**	licensed clerk in an
	industrial firm
heiraten	to marry
Die beiden haben geheiratet.	The two got married.
die **Schwiegereltern** (Pl.)	parents-in-law
die **Abteilung**, Abteilungen	department
die **Marketing-**	marketing department
Abteilung, -Abteilungen	
die **Sendung**, Sendungen	broadcast, show on radio
	or TV
die **Fernsehsendung**,	television show
-sendungen	
Amnesty International	Amnesty International
(ai)	
mitmachen	to participate, to be part of
Da will ich mitmachen.	I want to be part of that.
mitarbeiten	to collaborate, to work
	together (with)
der **Zufall**, Zufälle	accident, chance
Es war kein Zufall.	It was no accident.
Chile	Chile
betreuen	to see to the needs of,
	to take care of
politische Gefangene in	to take care of political
Chile betreuen	prisoners in Chile
geboren	born
Wo bist du geboren?	Where were you born?
aufwachsen	to grow up
als	as
eine Ausbildung als Industrie-	to do vocational training
kauffrau machen	for a licensed industrial
	clerkship

A8

wovon?	(about/of) what?
Wovon träumt Gundi?	What does Gundi dream
	of?
dazu passen	to match, to fit

Welche Blätter passen dazu?	Which leaves match it?
nebeneinander	next to each other
zwei Leben nebeneinander	to live two lives next to
leben	each other
tagsüber	during the day
die **Werbung**	advertisement
die **Amnesty-Gruppe**,	Amnesty group
-Gruppen	
unfrei	unfree
sich immer unfreier fühlen	to feel more and more
	unfree
weiterleben	to go on living

A9

die **Firma**, Firmen	firm, company

A10

ziehen	to move
an einen anderen Ort ziehen	to move to another place
aufhören	to stop, to quit
Ich habe bei Mercedes	I quit my job at Mercedes.
aufgehört.	
Lateinamerika	Latin America
ziemlich	considerable
die **Schwierigkeit**,	difficulty
Schwierigkeiten	
ziemliche Schwierigkeiten	to have considerable
haben	difficulty, to have a lot of
	trouble
gewöhnen, sich	to get used to
sich an das Leben hier	to get used to the life here
gewöhnen	
die **Dritte Welt**	Third World
die **Menschenrechte** (Pl.)	human rights
die **Grünen** (Pl.)	the Greens
der **Bundestag**	Federal Diet (lower house
	of the German parlia-
	ment)
die **Mitarbeiterin**,	collaborator, colleague,
Mitarbeiterinnen	co-worker
die **Zwischenzeit**	meantime
in der Zwischenzeit	in the meantime
der **Landtag**	state parliament
Nordrhein-Westfalen	North Rhine – Westphalia
inzwischen	meanwhile
der **Sohn**, Söhne	son
das **Fremde**	the unfamiliar, the foreign
spannend	exciting
Das Fremde kann spannend	The foreign can be ex-
und schön sein.	citing and beautiful.

A11

die **Handlung**,	action, act
Handlungen	
die **Entscheidung**,	decision
Entscheidungen	

A12

verh<u>ei</u>ratet	married
Bist du verheiratet?	Are you married?
ledig	single
unbedingt	definitely, no matter what
realis<u>ie</u>ren	to realize, to make real

4 Aussprache

A13

die **W-Frage**, W-Fragen	*wh*-question (including *how*-questions)

A14

letzt-	last, final
die letzte Silbe	the final syllable
interviewen	to interview
herkommen	to be from
Wo kommt Gundi her?	Where is Gundi from?

A15

die **Elimination**	elimination
unbetont	unstressed
die **Endsilbe**, Endsilben	final syllable
wegfallen	to be omitted, to be left out
Das unbetonte „e" kann in Endsilben wegfallen.	The unstressed "e" can be omitted in the final syllable.

A16

rhythmisch	rhythmical
anhalten	to stop

5 Wortschatz

A17

die **Wort-Familie**, -Familien	word family
fliegend	flying
Lesen Sie die „fliegenden" Wörter.	Read the "flying" words.
sinnlos	senseless
traumhaft	dreamlike, marvelous
friedlich	peaceful
unglücklich	unhappy
sicher	secure, safe

wünschen	to wish
sinnvoll	sensible
ungesund	unhealthy
die **Trauminsel**, -inseln	dream island
das **Lieblingsessen**	favorite food

A19

die **Station**, Stationen	station, stage, chapter
rekonstruieren	to reconstruct
Stationen einer Geschichte rekonstruieren	to reconstruct the chapters in a story
der **Kaufmann**	salesperson, clerk
verloben, sich	to become engaged
genießen	to enjoy
die Freizeit genießen	to enjoy one's leisure time
der **Verein**, Vereine	organization, club, association
bei einem Verein mitmachen	to be active in an association
verwirklichen	to make real, to realize
einen Traum verwirklichen	to realize a dream
der **Alltag**	everyday life
sich an den Alltag gewöhnen	to get used to everyday life
der **Mitarbeiter**, Mitarbeiter	collaborator, colleague, co-worker
die **Mitarbeiterin**, Mitarbeiterinnen	collaborator, colleague, co-worker

A20

aussuchen	to choose, to select
Suchen Sie Fotos aus.	Select photos.

6 Grammatik

der **Infinitiv**	infinitive
die **Infinitiv-Gruppe**, -Gruppen	infinitive group
entschließen, sich	to decide
das **Vollverb**, Vollverben	full verb
der **Demonstrativ-Artikel**	demonstrative pronoun
der **Stern**, Sterne	star
das **Tier**, Tiere	animal
begleiten	to accompany

18 Leben im Alter

1 Das Fotoalbum

das **Album**, Alben	album
das **Fotoalbum**, -alben	photo album

A1

ausschauen	to look, to appear
ängstlich	fearful, apprehensive
Sie schaut ängstlich aus.	She looks apprehensive.
interessiert	interested
selbstsicher	self-confident, self-assured
wirken	to seem, to give the impression
Sie wirkt auf mich sehr selbstsicher.	She gives me the impression of being very self-assured.

A2

geliebt	loved
heißgeliebt	fervently loved, dearly beloved
Meine heißgeliebte Johanna!	Dearly beloved Johanna,
da	because, as
Weihnachten	Christmas
Betracht	consideration
Ich falle außer Betracht.	I am no longer under consideration.
zurückschicken	to send back
die **Photographie**	photo
der **Gedanke**, Gedanken	thought
Ich bin in Gedanken stets bei dir.	My thoughts are always with you.
Alles Gute!	All the best!
der **Verehrer**, Verehrer	admirer
ein stiller Verehrer	a secret or silent admirer
die **Schwester**, Schwestern	sister

A3

der **Beruf**, Berufe	occupation, profession
Er war Politiker von Beruf.	He was a politician by profession.

2 Die Lebensalter früher und heute

A4

der **Bogen**, Bögen	sheet of paper
der **Bilderbogen**, -bögen	picture sheet, pictorial broadsheet
die **Uniform**, Uniformen	uniform
ein junger Mann in Uniform	a young man in uniform
verliebt	in love
sich verliebt in die Augen schauen	to look lovingly into each other's eyes
erreichen	to reach, to achieve
Sie haben viel erreicht.	They have achieved a great deal.
blicken	to look
nach vorn blicken	to look ahead
zurückblicken	to look back
der **Bart**, Bärte	beard
die **Geburt**, Geburten	birth
die **Kindheit**	childhood
die **Jugend**	youth
das **Erwachsensein**	adulthood, maturity
die **Heirat**	marriage
die **Macht**	power
das **Alter**	(old) age
ideal	ideal
das ideale Leben eines Paares im 19. Jahrhundert	the ideal life of a 19th-century couple
scheiden	to dissolve (marriage)
sich scheiden lassen	to get divorced

A5

die **Lebenstreppe**, -treppen	staircase of life

A6

die **Statistik**, Statistiken	statistic(s)
Statistik und Vortrag vergleichen	to compare the statistics and the presentation
die **Tabelle**, Tabellen	table
die Zahlen in der Tabelle	the numbers in the table
die **Kindersterblichkeit**	child mortality
lebend	alive
Kindersterblichkeit pro 1000 lebend geborenen Kindern	child mortality per 1000 children born alive
die **Anzahl**	number
die **Quote**, Quoten	proportion, rate
die **Scheidungsquote**, -quoten	divorce rate
europäisch	European
der **Durchschnitt**	average
die **Lebenserwartung**	life expectancy
der **Ruhestand**	retirement
die **Scheidung**, Scheidungen	divorce
die **Rate**, Raten	rate
die **Scheidungsrate**, -raten	divorce rate
Prozent	percent
Die Scheidungsrate lag bei 10 Prozent.	The divorce rate was 10 percent.
-jährig	-year-old
60-jährige Frauen	60-year-old women

3 ALTERnativen

die **Alternative**, Alternativen	alternative

A7

ausstoßen	to utter, to let out
der **Schrei**, Schreie	scream, cry
einen Schrei ausstoßen	to let out a cry
krachen	to crash, to bang
splittern	to splinter
die **Kante**, Kanten	edge
die **Handkante**	edge of the hand
schlagen	to strike, to hit, to break
das **Brett**, Bretter	board
das **Holzbrett**, -bretter	wooden board
ein Holzbrett in zwei Teile schlagen	to break a wooden board into two pieces
die **Teilnehmerin**, Teilnehmerinnen	participant
Wen-Do	wen-do
die **Seniorin**, Seniorinnen	senior citizen
ein Wen-Do Kurs für Seniorinnen	a wen-do course for female senior citizens

der **Kampfsport**	combative sport
die **Selbsterfahrung**	self-knowledge, learning about oneself
die **Verteidigung**	defense
die **Selbstverteidigung**	self-defense
die **Grauen Panther** (Pl.)	the Gray Panthers
organisieren	to organize
das **Mitglied**, Mitglieder	member
das **Enkelkind**, Enkel(kinder)	grandchild
der **Urenkel**, Urenkel	great-grandchild
die **Witwe**, Witwen	widow
engagieren, sich	to involve oneself
als sie sich bei den „Grauen Panthern" engagierte	when she got involved with the "Gray Panthers"
der **Dritte-Welt-Laden**, -Läden	Third-World store

A8

merken	to notice, to realize
befassen, sich	to concern oneself
Ich merke, es ist nötig, sich mit den Problemen zu befassen.	I realize that it is important to concern oneself with the problems.
darum	that is why, for this reason
Darum bin ich bei den „Grauen Panthern".	That is why I am with the "Gray Panthers."
das **Heim**, Heime	home
das **Altenheim**, -heime	old people's home
riesengroß	enormous, gigantic
der/die **Einsame**, die Einsamen	lonely person

4 Gespräch zwischen den Generationen

A10

die **Kurve**, Kurven	curve
Was kann diese Kurve bedeuten?	What can this curve mean?
die **Ahnung**, Ahnungen	notion, idea
Keine Ahnung!	I haven't the slightest idea!
darstellen	to represent
Für mich stellt die Kurve Beziehungen dar.	For me the curve represents relationships.

A11

sich Gedanken machen	to think about
der **Versuch**, Versuche	attempt
die **Verständigung**	understanding, communication
der **Verständigungsversuch**, -versuche	attempt at communication
die **Figur**, Figuren	figure
der **Gesprächsversuch**, -versuche	attempt at conversation

der **Hass**	hate
das **Verstehen**	understanding
das **Nicht-Verstehen**	absence or lack of understanding
selber	oneself, myself
das **Echo**	echo, resonance, response
Ich spüre kein Echo.	I don't feel any response.
dahin	there
Dahin kommt man mit 40.	You get there at 40.
die **Persönlichkeit**	personality
die eigene Persönlichkeit	one's own personality
überzeugen	to convince
Ich bin überzeugt, dass...	I am convinced that...

A12

entwerfen	to design, to draw
Bilder entwerfen	to draw pictures

A13

der **Hof**, Höfe	yard, courtyard
ausdenken, sich	to think up, to make up
sich eine eigene Sprache ausdenken	to make up one's own private language
toll	loud, with gusto
Alle beide lachten ganz toll.	Both laughed with great gusto
ober-	upper
im oberen Stockwerk des Hauses	on the upper floor of the house
der **Balkon**, Balkons	balcony
gegenüber	opposite
hinausschauen	to look out
erstaunt	astonished
ein erstauntes Gesicht machen	to look astonished
schweigen	to fall or remain silent
die **Geheimsprache**, -sprachen	secret language
weitersprechen	to continue to speak
lächelnd	smiling
froh	glad
Wie sind wir doch froh, dass...	We really are glad that...
nachdenken	to think, to reflect

5 Aussprache

A14

die **Kontrolle**, Kontrollen	check, control
weiterhören	to continue to listen
jammern	to moan, to lament
klagen	to complain

A15

der **Substantiv-Ausdruck**, -Ausdrücke	noun expression

die **Kinderzahl**	number of children
der **Seniorinnenkurs**, -kurse	course for female senior citizens

6 Wortschatz

A16

die **Tochter**, Töchter	daughter
die **Enkelin**, Enkelinnen	granddaughter
der **Enkel**, Enkel	grandson
die **Schwiegermutter**, -mütter	mother-in-law
der **Schwiegervater**, -väter	father-in-law
die **Geschwister** (Pl.)	brothers and sisters
die **Nichte**, Nichten	niece
der **Neffe**, Neffen	nephew
die **Tante**, Tanten	aunt
der **Onkel**, Onkel	uncle
die **Großeltern** (Pl.)	grandparents
die **Großmutter**, -mütter	grandmother
der **Großvater**, -väter	grandfather

7 Grammatik

das **Tempus**	tense
die **Tempusform**, -formen	tense form
Tempusformen der Verben	tense forms of the verbs
zusammen sein (mit)	to be together (with)
vorbei	over, past
Das ist vorbei.	That's over.
mündlich	oral
schriftlich	written
der **Präsens-Stamm**	present-stem
der **Präteritum-Stamm**	past-stem
brennen	to burn
senden	to send
wenden	to turn
das **Merkwort**, Merkwörter	mnemonic word, memory aid
das **Einzelverb**, Einzelverben	individual verb
rufen	to call, to shout
der **Temporalsatz**, Temporalsätze	time clause
gleichzeitig	simultaneous
gleichzeitige Temporalsätze	simultaneous time clauses
die **Vergangenheit**	past
einmalig	single, non-recurring
eine einmalige Handlung	a non-recurring action
wiederholt	repeated
ein wiederholtes Ereignis	a repeated occurrence
der **Genitiv**	genitive
das **Bezugswort**, Bezugswörter	modified word, head (of genitive)
der **Personenname**, -namen	(personal) name

19 Umwelt

die **Umwelt**	environment

1 Alles dreht sich...

A2

der **Mond**	moon
fantastisch	fantastic
ein fantastisches Erlebnis	a fantastic experience
die **Erde**	earth
beeindrucken	to impress
Mich beeindruckt, wie schön diese Erde ist.	I'm impressed by how beautiful this earth is.
winzig	tiny
unermesslich	immeasurable
wie eine winzige Insel in einem unermesslichen Meer	like a tiny island in an immeasurable sea
soweit	as far as
soweit wir wissen	as far as we know
bewusst werden	to become aware
mir ist bewusst geworden	I have become aware
erhalten	to maintain
bewahren	to preserve
der **Angreifer**, Angreifer	attacker
vor fremden Angreifern schützen	to protect from alien attackers
der **Astronaut**, Astronauten	astronaut
kaputtmachen	to ruin, to destroy
roden	to uproot
vergiften	to poison
fangen	to catch
feststellen	to ascertain, to see
indianisch	Indian
die **Weisheit**, Weisheiten	wisdom, proverb
indianische Weisheit	American Indian proverb

A3

die **Faszination**	fascination
wovor?	of what?
Wovor hast du Angst?	What are you afraid of?
fürchten	to fear

Was fürchten Sie?	What do you fear?
die **Sorge**, Sorgen	worry, care
sich Sorgen machen	to worry
deiner Meinung nach	in your opinion
unternehmen	to undertake, to do
weitermachen	to continue, to keep on
am meisten	the most
faszinierend	fascinating

2 Der Wasserkreislauf

A4

das **Wasserproblem**, -probleme	water problem
erklären	to explain
der **Kreislauf**, Kreisläufe	cycle
der **Wasserkreislauf**	water cycle
nachzeichnen	to trace
erwärmen	to warm
verdunsten	to evaporate
aufsteigen	to rise
so dass	so that, with the result that
die **Regenwolke**, -wolken	raincloud
abkühlen	to cool
Die Wolken werden in der Höhe abgekühlt.	High in the sky the clouds are cooled.
schneien	to snow
Es regnet und schneit.	It rains and snows.
die **Pflanze**, Pflanzen	plant
sammeln (sich)	to accumulate
der **Bach**, Bäche	stream, brook
Wasser sammelt sich in den Bächen.	Water accumulates in the brooks.
zurückfließen	to flow back
Das Wasser fließt zurück ins Meer.	The water flows back into the sea.
von vorne	from the beginning
von vorne beginnen	to start again from the beginning

A5

sauber	clean
der **Boden** , Böden	earth, soil
die **Chemikalie**, Chemikalien	chemical
Der Boden wird mit Chemikalien behandelt.	The soil is treated with chemicals.
giftig	poisonous, toxic
der **Stoff**, Stoffe	substance
giftige Stoffe	toxic substances

A6

das **Grundwasser**	ground water
Das Grundwasser wird vergiftet, so dass...	The ground water becomes poisoned, so that...

die **Lage**	situation
verbessern, sich	to improve
verschlechtern, sich	to get worse, to deteriorate
Die Lage hat sich verbessert/verschlechtert.	The situation has improved/deteriorated.

3 Was tun Sie für die Umwelt?

A7

das **Verhalten**	behavior
das **Umweltverhalten**	environmental behavior
die **Verschmutzung**, Verschmutzungen	pollution
die **Luftverschmutzung**	air pollution
die **Wasserverschmut-zung**	water pollution
das **Ozon**	ozone
das **Ozonloch**	ozone hole
der **Müll**	refuse, waste, garbage
der **Müllberg**, -berge	mountain of garbage
alltäglich	daily, everyday
ein alltägliches Thema	an everyday topic
die **Energie**	energy
Energie sparen	to conserve energy
damit	in order that
sparsam	thrifty, economical
umgehen (mit)	to deal with, to treat, to use
sparsam mit Energie umgehen	to use energy economically
die **Chance**, Chancen	chance
der **Eimer**, Eimer	bucket, can
der **Mülleimer**, -eimer	dustbin, garbage can
wegwerfen	to throw away
die **Illusion**, Illusionen	illusion
sich keine Illusionen machen	to not delude oneself
kaputtgehen	to break down, to go to ruin

A8

der **Schutz**	protection
der Schutz der Natur	the protection of nature
dagegen sein	to be against something, to oppose

A9

der **Umweltschutz**	environmental protection
konkret	concrete, actual
Was tust du konkret im Alltag?	What do you actually do in your daily life?
verbrauchen	to consume, to use
dafür sein, dass ...	to be in favor of ...
zum Glück	fortunately

4 Das Auto der Zukunft oder Zukunft ohne Auto?

A10

Pro	pro
Kontra	con
Pro und Kontra diskutieren	to discuss the pros and cons
das **Argument**, Argumente	argument
mobil	mobile
die **Gesellschaft**	society
eine mobile Gesellschaft	a mobile society
die **Mobilität**	mobility
das beste Mittel für individuelle Mobilität	the best means of individual mobility
bereit sein	to be prepared
das **Einkommen**	income
das **Autofahren**	driving an automobile
ausgeben	to spend
die **Industrie**, Industrien	industry
die **Automobilindustrie**	automotive industry
der **Faktor**, Faktoren	factor
der **Wirtschaftsfaktor**, -faktoren	economic factor
der Wirtschaftsfaktor Nummer 1	Economic Factor No. 1
die **Million**, Millionen	million
das **Fahrzeug**, Fahrzeuge	vehicle
das **Kraftfahrzeug**, Kraftfahrzeuge	motor vehicle
Es gibt 52 Millionen Kraftfahrzeuge.	There are 52 million motor vehicles.
der **Feind**, Feinde	enemy
der größte Feind des Autos	the greatest enemy of the automobile
untergehen	to sink, to go under, to disappear
Andere Produkte gehen unter.	Other products disappear.
in Schwierigkeiten kommen	to run into difficulties
das **Automobil**, Automobile	automobile
befriedigen	to satisfy
perfekt	perfect
Wünsche perfekt befriedigen	to completely satisfy wishes
verzichten (auf)	to do without
Niemand will auf das Auto verzichten.	Nobody wants to do without his or her car.
die **Auswirkung**, Auswirkungen	effect
verbringen	to spend (time etc.)
der **Autofahrer**, Autofahrer	motorist
Deutsche Autofahrer verbringen im Durchschnitt pro Jahr drei Tage im Stau.	German motorists spend an average of three days per year in a traffic jam.
das **Aussteigen**	getting out (here meant figuratively: not using the car)
lösen	to solve
das **Verkehrsproblem**, -probleme	traffic problem
die **Beschränkung**, Beschränkungen	restriction
die **Kreativität**	creativity
der **Minister**, Minister	minister
der **Bundesminister**, -minister	federal minister
die **Forschung**, Forschungen	research
die **Technologie**	technology
der Bundesminister für Forschung und Technologie	German Federal Minister for Research and Technology
der **Aussteiger**, Aussteiger	dropout

A11

das **Verkehrsmittel**, Verkehrsmittel	means of transportation
die **Versuchsperson**, Versuchspersonen	test subject, test person
stehen lassen	to leave standing, to leave parked
der **Pkw**, Pkws (= Personenkraftwagen)	automobile
der **Privatwagen**, -wagen	private automobile
die **Wienerin**, Wienerinnen	Viennese woman
der **Wiener**, Wiener	Viennese man
das **Fahrrad**, Fahrräder	bicycle
das **Car-Sharing** (engl.)	car-sharing
mit öffentlichen Verkehrsmitteln, Fahrrad und Car-Sharing mobil bleiben	to stay mobile with public transportation, bicycles, and car-sharing
das **Ergebnis**, Ergebnisse	result, findings
vorliegen	to be now available
Das Ergebnis des Versuches liegt vor.	The findings of the study are now available.
verkaufen	to sell
die **Analyse**, Analysen	analysis
die Analyse zeigt, dass ...	the analysis shows that ...
während	during
während des Versuchs	during the investigation
reduzieren, sich	to be reduced
der **Anteil**, Anteile	share, proportion

Der Anteil reduzierte sich auf drei Prozent.	The share was reduced to three percent.
die **Freizeit-Fahrt**, Freizeit-Fahrten	leisure-time driving, Sunday drive
hingegen	on the other hand

A12

sprechen	to speak
Für/Gegen das Auto spricht, dass..	It speaks for/against the automobile that . . .
dringend	urgent
es ist dringend nötig	it is urgent(ly necessary)
gleicher Meinung wie jemand anderer sein	to be of the same opinion as someone else
zustimmen	to agree

5 Aussprache

A13

die **Entscheidungsfrage**, -fragen	decisive question
das **Car-Sharing-Projekt**, -Projekte	car-sharing project

A14

schaden	to harm, to damage
reinigen	to clean
das **Gift**, Gifte	poison

A15

die **Assimilation**	assimilation
gehoben	elevated
die gehobene Sprache	elevated language
die **Alltagssprache**	ordinary speech
assimilieren	to assimilate

6 Wortschatz

A16

die **Assoziation**, Assoziationen	association
assoziieren	to associate
Was assoziieren Sie zu den markierten Wörtern?	What do you associate with the words marked in blue?
problematisch	problematical
missbrauchen	to misuse
verschmutzt	polluted
verschmutztes Öl	polluted oil
schmutzig	dirty
baden	to swim, to bathe
Das Baden für Menschen muss verboten werden.	Bathing has to be prohibited for humans.
das **Trinkwasser**	drinking water
das **Recycling**	recycling
lebensgefährlich	life-threatening

A17

gesucht	wanted
Wörter gesucht	words wanted
der **Steckbrief**, Steckbriefe	"wanted" poster
die **Eigenschaft**, Eigenschaften	characteristic
schlechte Eigenschaften	negative characteristics
die **Fabrik**, Fabriken	factory
der **Dünger**, Dünger	fertilizer

A18

produzieren	to produce
die **Verpackung**	packaging
die **Batterie**, Batterien	battery
der **Atommüll**	atomic waste
das **Abwasser**, Abwässer	sewage
der **Strom**	electricity
der **Abfall**, Abfälle	refuse, waste
die **Giftstoffe** (Pl.)	toxic substances
die **Abgase** (Pl.)	emissions, exhaust
das **Benzin**	gasoline

A19

bis	until
dran sein	to have a turn
Spielen Sie, bis alle Verben einmal dran waren.	Play until all the verbs have had one turn.

7 Grammatik

das **Passiv**	passive
das **Vorgangspassiv**	actional passive
die **Verbform**, Verbformen	verb form
das **Aktiv**	active
die **Bildung**	formation
die Bildung des Passiv	formation of the passive
das **Hilfsverb**, Hilfsverben	auxiliary verb
erweitert	extended
erweitertes Passiv	agentive passive, passive with an agent
der **Urheber**, Urheber	agent
leiten	to conduct, to channel
Abwässer ins Meer leiten	to channel sewage into the sea
verbieten	to forbid, to prohibit
der **Vorgang**	process
statt	instead of
das **Indefinitpronomen**	indefinite pronoun
der **Konsekutivsatz**, -sätze	consecutive clause
der **Finalsatz**, -sätze	purpose clause
die **Maßnahme**, Maßnahmen	measure
der **Zweck**, Zwecke	purpose

1 Reise-Impressionen

die **Impression**, Impressionen	impression
die **Reise-Impression**, -Impressionen	travel impressions

A1

das **Reisebild**, -bilder	travel sketch
das **Reisegefühl**, -gefühle	travel feeling
der **Sinn**, Sinne	sense, mind
Was kommt Ihnen in den Sinn?	What comes into your mind?

A2

1

die **Betrachtung**, Betrachtungen	observation
die **Reisebetrachtung**, -betrachtungen	travel observation
heutig	today's, contemporary
die **Kutsche**, Kutschen	coach
die **Postkutsche**, -kutschen	mail coach
Die Reisebetrachtungen Goethes wurden aus einer Postkutsche gemacht.	Goethe's travel observations were made from a mail coach.
das **Gelände**, Gelände	terrain, landscape
entwickeln, sich	to develop
Sie entwickeln sich mit der langsamen Veränderung des Geländes.	They develop with the slowly changing landscape.

2

das **Reisen**	travel
zappen	to zap
Sie „zappen" durchs Leben.	They "zap" through life.
der **Last-Minute-Flug**, -Flüge	last-minute flight
die **Destination**, Destinationen	destination
im Last-Minute-Flug von Destination zu Destination	in the last-minute flight from destination to destination

3

der **D-Zug**, D-Züge	express train
manch-	many a, some
schnittig	streamlined, stylish, smart
der **Achtzylinder** (= der Achtzylinder-Wagen)	eight-cylinder car
Mancher findet nur schnittige Achtzylinder schön.	Some find only eight-cylinder cars attractive.
meinerseits	for my part
sehnsuchtsvoll	full of longing
seit langen sehnsuchtsvollen Jahren	for long years full of longing
die **Schwäche**, Schwächen	weakness
rauchgrau	smoke-gray
die **Schlange**, Schlangen	snake, serpentine
eine Schwäche für rauchgraue D-Zug-Schlangen haben	to have a weakness for smoke-gray express-train serpentines
entlegen	remote, distant

4

das **Los**, Lose	lot, lottery ticket
das große Los gewinnen	to win the lottery
gut tun	to be good for someone

5

irren, sich	to be wrong
528 Millionen Touristen können sich nicht irren.	528 million tourists can't be wrong.
die **Ankunft**, Ankünfte	arrival
der **Tourismus**	tourism
die **Welttourismus-Organisation**	World Tourism Organization
vergangen	past, last
Die Welttourismus-Organisation zählte im vergangenen Jahr 528 Millionen Ankünfte.	Last year the World Tourism Organization counted 528 million arrivals.
fragen, sich	to ask oneself
ernsthaft	serious
ob	whether
solch-	such
Masse, Massen	mass
Ich frage mich ernsthaft, ob das Reisen bei solchen Massen noch schön ist?	I seriously ask myself whether travel is still enjoyable among such masses of people.

6

blühen	to bloom
das Land, wo die Zitronen blühen	the land where the lemon trees bloom
das **Laub**	foliage
die **Goldorange**, -orangen	golden orange
glühen	to glow
wo im dunkeln Laub die Gold-Orangen glühen	where the golden oranges glow in the dark foliage
die **Myrte**, Myrten	myrtle
die Myrte steht still	the myrtle stands silent
der **Lorbeer**, Lorbeeren	laurel
der Lorbeer steht hoch	the laurel stands high
dahin	to that place, there
der/die **Geliebte**	love(r), beloved
o!	O!
ziehen	to journey, to go
Dahin möchte ich mit dir, o mein Geliebter, ziehen.	There I would like to go with you, O my beloved.

7

aufs (= auf das)	for
verwenden	to use, to spend
Zeit und Kraft aufs Fliegen verwenden	to spend time and energy for flying
für	for, after
Bild für Bild	picture after picture
ans (= an das)	of
das **Verkaufen**	selling
nicht ans Verkaufen denken	to not think of selling

A3

kommentieren	to comment on
Kommentieren Sie Ihre Collagen.	Comment on your collages.

A4

bewegen	to move, to motivate
Was bewegt die Menschen?	What motivates people?
verreisen	to go on trips, to travel
langweilen	to bore
Langweilt der Alltag die Menschen?	Does everyday life bore people?
anziehen	to attract
Ziehen uns fremde Menschen an?	Do foreign people attract us?
die **Ferne**	faraway places
Was ist es, das die Menschen in die Ferne zieht?	What is it that attracts people to faraway places?
der **Mount Everest**	Mount Everest
fern	distant
die **Südseeinsel**, -inseln	South Sea island
das **Wohnmobil**, -mobile	camper

2 Heinrich Heine: Reisebilder (1822–28)

A5

Tirol	Tirol

A6

1

fort	away
fort, fort von hier	away, away from here

2

preußisch	Prussian
kreuz und quer	all over, all around
durchstreifen	to roam
den preußischen Teil Polens kreuz und quer durchstreifen	to roam all over the Prussian part of Poland
die **Fläche**, Flächen	area, expanse
das **Ackerland**	farmland
weite Flächen und Ackerland	vast expanses and farmland
der **Fichtenwald**, -wälder	spruce forest
leben (von)	to live from

der **Ackerbau**	farming
die **Viehzucht**	livestock breeding
Polen lebt nur von Ackerbau und Viehzucht.	Poland lives only from farming and livestock breeding.
die **Spur**, Spuren	trace
Es gibt keine Spur von Fabriken und Industrie.	There is no trace of factories and industry.

3

die **Krone**, Kronen	crown
der **Harz**	the Harz (Mountains)
in der „Krone" zu Klausthal im Harz zu Mittag essen	to have lunch in the "Crown" at Klausthal in the Harz
frühlingsgrün	spring-green
die **Petersiliensuppe**, -suppen	parsely soup
veilchenblau	violet
der **Kohl**	cabbage
sowie	as well
die **Art**, Arten	type, kind
geräuchert	smoked
der **Hering**, Heringe	herring
sowie auch eine Art geräucherte Heringe	as well as a kind of smoked herring
der **Bückling**, Bücklinge	kipper
sich auf den Weg machen	to set out for, to proceed
die **Grube**, Gruben	pit, mine
die **Harzreise**	journey through the Harz

4

der **Einwohner**, Einwohner	inhabitant
friesisch	Frisian
die Einwohner der friesischen Insel Norderney	inhabitants of the Frisian island of Norderney
bleich	pale
der **Fischfang**	fishing
dienen	to serve
der **Matrose**, Matrosen	sailor, seaman
Viele dienen als Matrosen auf fremden Schiffen.	Many serve as seamen on foreign ships.
jahrelang	for years (at a time)
entfernt bleiben	to be away from
der/die **Angehörige**, die Angehörigen	relative
die **Nachricht**, Nachrichten	news
zukommen lassen	to send to
Sie bleiben oft jahrelang von zu Hause entfernt, ohne ihren Angehörigen eine Nachricht von sich zukommen zu lassen.	They are often away from home for years at a time without sending news of themselves to their relatives.

5

erfr**eu**en	to give pleasure
tr**ü**b	gloomy
die **Witterung**	weather
die **Gemütsstimmung**, -stimmungen	mood, state of mind
d**a**nn und w**a**nn	now and then
der **Wagen**, Wagen/ Wägen	wagon, coach
himmelhoch	as high as the sky
Dann schaute ich himmel- hohe Berge.	Then I saw mountains towering into the sky.

6

wegen	because of, on account of
das **Sprechen**	speech, speaking
das **Italienischsprechen**	speaking Italian
h**a**lten (für)	to take for
der **Engländer**, Engländer	Englishman
Wegen meines Italienisch- sprechens hielt sie mich für einen Engländer.	Because of the way I spoke Italian they took me for an Englishman.
sogl**ei**ch	immediately
ökon**o**misch	economic
klim**a**tisch	climatic
w**a**chsen	to grow
. . . , dass keine Zitronen wachsen	. . . that no lemons grow

7

zahlreich	numerous
durchzi**e**hen	to travel through
der **Schwarm**, Schwärme	swarm, horde
Sie durchziehen dieses Land in ganzen Schwärmen.	They travel through this country in absolute hordes.
das **Wirtshaus**, -häuser	inn
umh**e**rlaufen	to run around
der **Zitronenbaum**, -bäume	lemon tree
die **Engländerin**, Engländerinnen	Englishwoman
ri**e**chen	to smell
Man kann sich keinen Zitronenbaum denken ohne eine Engländerin, die daran riecht.	You can't imagine a lemon tree without an English- woman smelling it.

A7

das **Stichwort**, Stichworte	catchword, keyword
die **Region**, Regionen	region

A8

aktuell	of current interest, topical
Welche Texte sind noch aktuell?	Which texts are still topi- cal?

3 Auf Heines Spuren

A9

die **Biografie**, Biografien	biography
jüdisch	Jewish
als Kind jüdischer Eltern	the child of Jewish parents
das **Gymnasium**, Gymnasien	university-preparatory high school
die **Handelsschule**, -schulen	commercial college
das **Studium**	university studies
Jura	law
das **Jura-Studium**	law studies
der **Jurist**, Juristen	lawyer, jurist
der **Schriftsteller**, Schriftsteller	writer
der **Journalist**, Journalisten	journalist
unternehmen	to undertake, to go on
längere Reisen unternehmen	to go on longer journeys
emigri**e**ren	to emigrate
exponi**e**ren, sich	to lay oneself open to attack
Er exponierte sich politisch.	Politically, he laid himself open to attack.
die **Polizei**	police
liberal	liberal
die **Bewegung**, Bewegungen	movement
politische Bewegungen	political movements
einleben, sich	to make oneself at home, to grow accustomed to the life
das **Exil**	exile
die **Exil-Heimat**	country of exile, home in exile
Heine lebte sich schnell in der Exil-Heimat ein.	Heine quickly grew accustomed to life in his home in exile.
bekannt	well-known
der **Bürger**, Bürger	citizen
der **Weltbürger**, -bürger	citizen of the world
romantisch	romantic
ironisch	ironic
die **Lyrik**	lyric poetry
seine romantische ironische Lyrik	his romantic, ironic lyric poetry
kritisch	critical
seine modern-kritischen Reise-Impressionen	his travel impressions, which are quite modern in their criticism

A10

der **Werbetext**, -texte	advertising copy
bestimmt	certain
ein bestimmter Ort	a certain place

A

der **Gourmet**, Gourmets	gourmet
Gourmet-Tage	gourmet days
die **Anreise**	journey to a place
die **Übernachtung**, Übernachtungen	overnight stay
das **Frühstücksbuffet**, -buffets	breakfast buffet
der **Cocktail**, Cocktails	cocktail
der **Begrüßungscocktail**, -cocktails	complimentary welcoming cocktail
das **Bergwerk**, Bergwerke	mine
das **Bergwerksmuseum**, -museen	mine museum
die **Wanderkarte**, -karten	(hiking) trailmap
die **Autokarte**, -karten	roadmap
das **Hallenbad**, -bäder	indoor swimming pool
1x freier Eintritt in das Hallenbad	one free admission to the indoor swimming pool
der **Gang**, Gänge	course
ein 5-Gang-Gourmetmenü	a five-course gourmet dinner
inklusive	including
der **Aperitif**, Aperitifs	aperitif
rustikal	rustic, country
die **Haxe**, Haxen	shank
ein rustikales Haxenessen	a country shank dinner
das **Licht**, Lichter	light
das **Grubenlicht**, -lichter	miner's lamp
das **Doppelzimmer**, -zimmer	double room

B

Ostfriesland	East Frisian Islands
das **Abendessen**, -essen	evening meal, dinner
mondän	fashionable, sophisticated
die **Badeinsel**, -inseln	island bathing resort
die mondäne Badeinsel in der Nordsee	the sophisticated island bathing resort in the North Sea
die **Faust**, Fäuste	fist
auf eigene Faust	on one's own initiative
erkunden	to explore
die Insel auf eigene Faust erkunden	to explore the island on one's own

C

die **Lagune**, Lagunen	lagoon
die Lagunenstadt Venedig	the lagoon city of Venice
die **Tauern** (Pl.)	Tauern Mountains
die **Tauern-Autobahn**	Tauern Highway
das **Motorboot**, -boote	motorboat
die **Stadtführung**, -führungen	city tour
der **Palast**, Paläste	palace
der Dogenpalast	Palace of the Doges
die **Seufzerbrücke**	Bridge of Sighs
usw. (= und so weiter)	etc., and so on
anschließend	afterward
die **Verfügung**	disposal, availability
zur freien Verfügung	free
die **Rückreise**	return journey
Abf. (= Abfahrt)	departure
inkl. (= inklusive)	including

4 Wenn einer eine Reise tut, dann kann er was erzählen ...

A12

der **Zoll**, Zölle	customs, duties
reagieren	to react
Wie reagieren Sie in einer solchen Situation?	How do you react in such a situation?

1

wechseln	to exchange
Wo kann ich hier Geld wechseln, bitte?	Where can I exchange money here, please?
der **Scheck**, Schecks	check
Nehmen die da auch Schecks?	Do they also take checks?

2

Griechenland	Greece
der **Pfennig**, Pfennige	penny, pfennig
die **Marke**, Marken	postage stamp
Geben Sie mir bitte 5 Marken zu 80 Pfennig.	Please give me five 80-pfennig stamps.
oh!	Oh!

3

tun	to do
Was kann ich für Sie tun?	What can I do for you?
stehlen	to steal
der **Geldbeutel**, -beutel	purse
aha!	Aha!
Aha, weg war er!	Aha, it was gone!

4

die **Papiere** (Pl.)	papers, documents
Ihre Papiere bitte.	Your documents, please.
verzollen	to declare (for customs)
Haben Sie etwas zu verzollen?	Have you anything to declare?

A13

der/die **Beamte**, die Beamten	official
bemerken	to notice

5 Aussprache

A14

der **Kontrastakzent**	contrast accent
das **Kontrastwort**, -wörter	contrast word

A16

das **Wintermärchen**	winter's tale
grüßen	to greet
lind	soft, gentle
labend	soothing
Die Luft war lind und labend.	The air was soft and soothing.

6 Wortschatz

A17

einfallen	to occur to, to think of
Was fällt Ihnen noch ein?	What else can you think of?
der **Park**, Parks	park
der **Gasthof**, -höfe	restaurant, inn
der **Stock**, Stöcke	walking stick

7 Grammatik

der **Relativsatz**, -sätze	relative clause
das **Relativpronomen**	relative pronoun
identisch	identical
einleiten	to introduce
beziehen, sich	to refer to
die **Bezeichnung**, Bezeichnungen	designation
die **Ortsbezeichnung**, -bezeichnungen	place name
indirekt	indirect
der **Fragesatz**, -sätze	question clause
der indirekte Fragesatz	indirect question clause
informieren, sich	to inform oneself
die **Quantität**	quantity
der **Umstand**, Umstände	circumstance
die **Begründung**, Begründungen	reason, grounds

21 Heimat

1 Wie man eine Stadt liest

A3

die **Seele**, Seelen	soul
Was ist die Seele einer Stadt?	What is the soul of this city?

A4

das **Element**, Elemente	element
Elemente aus dem Text	elements from the text
der **Sinn**, Sinne	sense
mit allen Sinnen	with all five senses
die **Träne**, Tränen	tear
das **Lachen**	laughter, laughing
der/die **Verliebte**, die Verliebten	person in love
umarmen	to embrace
zwei Verliebte, die sich umarmen	two lovers who embrace
streiten	to fight, to quarrel
die **Steintreppe**, -treppen	stone steps
hinuntersteigen	to climb down
zuschauen	to watch, to look at
wandern	to wander
die Gedanken wandern lassen, nichts tun	to do nothing but let one's thoughts wander
der **Geruch**, Gerüche	smell
das **Gewürz**, Gewürze	spice
exotisch	exotic
exotische Früchte	exotic fruits
die **Melancholie**	melancholy
nach und nach	gradually, little by little
erleben, wie nach und nach die Lichter angehen	to experience the lights gradually going on

A5

der **Stadtplaner**, -planer	city planner
die **Entwicklung**, Entwicklungen	development

2 Freiburg/Fribourg- eine zweisprachige Stadt?

zweisprachig	bilingual

A6

offiziell	official
die **Bevölkerung**	population
etwa 30 % der Bevölkerung	about 30 % of the population
der **Ausländer**, Ausländer	foreigner
die **Ausländerin**, Ausländerinnen	foreigner
Portugiesisch	Portuguese
der **Straßenname**, -namen	street name

A7

1

das **Sprichwort**, -wörter	proverb
deutlich	clear
Ich merke es ganz deutlich bei mir.	I notice it quite clearly in myself.

2

die **Kultur**, Kulturen	culture

Mir gefallen die verschiedenen Menschen und Kulturen.	I like the different people and cultures.
der **Indio**, Indios	Indio
w**o**hl f**ü**hlen, sich	to feel good or comfortable
spont**a**n	spontaneous
Ich wünsche mir, die Leute wären ein bisschen spontaner.	I wish the people were a little more spontaneous.

3

das **Elsass**	Alsace

A8

argument**ie**ren	to argue
eher	sooner, rather
Nein, ich möchte eher in . . . leben.	No, I would rather live in . . .
wom**i**t?	with what?
Womit hättest du Probleme?	What would you have problems with?

A9

die **M**ehrsprachigkeit	multilingualism
Mehrsprachigkeit entdecken	to discover multilingualism
m**e**hrsprachig	multilingual
das **Schild**, Schilder	sign
die **Sprachlandschaft**, -landschaften	language landscape

3 Was ist Heimat?

A10

umschr**ei**ben	to paraphrase, to describe
einen Begriff umschreiben	to describe a concept
die **Vorstellung**, Vorstellungen	idea
verst**e**hen	to understand
Jeder versteht unter dem Wort „Heimat" etwas anderes.	Everyone understands something different with the word "Heimat" (home, homeland etc.).
der **Pol**itiker, Politiker	politician
der **Demonstrant**, Demonstranten	demonstrator
der **Bauer**, Bauern	farmer
der **Moment**, Momente	moment
schöne Momente aus der Kindheit	fond moments from childhood
die **Gegend**, Gegenden	region, area
der **Lauf**	course
im Lauf(e) des Lebens	in the course of one's life

A11

geh**ö**ren zu	to belong to, to be part of
Was gehörte für Sie früher zur Heimat?	What used to be part of "home" for you?

1

die **Fahne**, Fahnen	flag
der **Pass**, Pässe	passport
die **Hymne**, Hymnen	hymn, anthem
die **Nationalhymne**, -hymnen	national anthem
der **Feiertag**, -tage	holiday
der **Nationalfeiertag**, -tage	national holiday

2

das **Vaterland**	nation, country

3

die **Vogelstimme**, -stimmen	bird's voice

4

die **Kochkunst**, -künste	culinary art

A

die **Verbundenheit**	closeness, attachment
ein Gefühl der Verbundenheit mit der Familie	a feeling of belonging or of closeness to the family

C

ausdr**ü**cken, sich	to express oneself
Ich kann mich gut ausdrücken.	I can express myself well.

D

h**ei**matlos	without a home(land), nationless
defin**ie**ren	to define
Wie würden Sie Heimat definieren?	How would you define "home(land)"?

4 „Wenn ich keine Heimat hätte . . ."

A13

A

das **Vorurteil**, Vorurteile	prejudice
Der Mensch würde vielleicht mit weniger Vorurteilen leben.	People would perhaps live with fewer prejudices.
Kro**a**tien	Croatia

B

derj**e**nige	the one who/which/where etc.
aus demjenigen Ort, wo . . .	from that place where . . .
das **Daheimgefühl**	feeling of home
Lettland	Latvia

C

die **Identität**, Identitäten	identity
Es gäbe kein Land zu verteidigen.	There would be no country to defend.
der **Iran**	Iran

5 Aussprache

A14

der **Gaumen**	palate

A15

tr**e**nnen	to separate
der **Kn**a**cklaut**, -laute	glottal stop
kn**a**cken	to crack, to snap, to pop
h**ö**rbar	audible

6 Wortschatz

A16

v**a**ge	vague
vage Aussagen machen	to make vague statements
der **Dial**e**kt**, Dialekte	dialect
die **Spr**a**chgrenze**,	language boundary
-grenzen	
in e**twa**	approximately

A17

die **Erkl**ä**rung**,	explanation
Erklärungen	

der **S**a**tzanfang**,	beginning of the sentence
-anfänge	

7 Grammatik

der **K**o**njunktiv II**	past subjunctive
der **Indikativ**	indicative
die **Hyp**o**these**,	hypothesis
Hypothesen	
irreal	unreal
die **F**o**rm**, Formen	form
die **Umschr**e**ibung**,	paraphrase
Umschreibungen	
die **K**o**njunktiv II –**	paraphrase with the past
Umschreibung	subjunctive
id**e**ntisch	identical
der **B**ä**r**, Bären	bear

22 Medien und Informationen

die **M**e**dien** (Pl.)	the media

1 Wie funktioniert das?

A1

das **Ger**ä**t**, Geräte	appliance, device
die **Funktion**,	function
Funktionen	
Geräte und Funktionen	to describe devices and
beschreiben	functions
tr**a**gbar	portable
der **CD-Player**, Player	CD player
der tragbare CD-Player	portable CD player
j**o**ggen	to jog
die **St**e**ckdose**, -dosen	socket
ultra-	ultra-
ultraspa**rsam**	ultra-economical
superle**icht**	super lightweight
der **K**o**pfhörer**, -hörer	earphones
garant**ie**ren	to guarantee
e**inlegen**	to insert, to put in
w**ä**hrend	while
schw**i**tzen	to sweat
Während andere im Büro	While others are sweating
schwitzen, ...	in the office ...
die **Fernbedienung**	remote control
die **Mini-Fernbedienung**	mini remote control
das **J**o**ggen**	jogging
beim Joggen durch Feld und	while jogging through
Wald	fields and woods
wor**aus**	of what
best**e**hen	consist

Woraus besteht ein	What does a CD player
CD-Player?	consist of?
funktion**ie**ren	to function, to work
Wie funktioniert das?	How does it work?
st**e**cken	to plug (in)

A2

das **Fax**, Faxe	fax
Wie funktioniert ein Fax-	How does a fax machine
Gerät?	work?
kop**ie**ren	to copy
die **Installation**	installation
der **St**e**cker**, Stecker	plug
der **Tel**e**fon-Anschluss-**	telephone connecting plug
stecker, -stecker	
die **Anschlussdose**, -dosen	connecting socket
die **Tel**e**fon-Anschluss-**	telephone connecting
dose, -dosen	socket
der **N**e**tzstecker**, -stecker	wall plug
die **N**e**tzsteckdose**, -dosen	wall socket
der **Sch**a**lter**, Schalter	switch
der **N**e**tzschalter**, -schalter	power switch
das **Dokument**,	document
Dokumente	
die **Schr**i**ft**, Schriften	writing
die **B**i**ldseite**, -seiten	picture side
mit der Schrift-/Bildseite	with the writing side/
nach unten	picture side face-down
der **E**i**nzug**	feeder
die **T**a**ste**, Tasten	key
Clear/Copy (engl.)	Clear/Copy
erst**e**llen	to make, to produce

automatisch	automatic
die **Kopie**, Kopien	copy
Das Gerät erstellt automatisch eine Kopie.	The device automatically produces a copy.

2 Wie leben Sie damit?

A3

nutzen	to use
Wie nutzt die Frau Radio und Fernsehen?	How does the woman use radio and television?
der **Fernseher**, Fernseher	television
anmachen	to turn on
Ich mache das Radio an.	I turn on the radio.
die **Nachricht**, Nachrichten	report, news
Info (kurz für: Information)	information
der **Moderator**, Moderatoren	moderator
ab und zu	now and then
der **Film**, Filme	film
der **Spielfilm**, -filme	feature film, fiction film
die **Reportage**, Reportagen	report, reporting
der **Krimi**, Krimis	crime show
das **Hörspiel**, Hörspiele	radio play
die **Informationssendung**, -sendungen	information broadcast

A4

das **Freizeit-Magazin**, -Magazine	leisure-time magazine or section (in newspapers)
der **Experte**, Experten	expert
der **Alarm**	alarm
Experten schlagen Alarm.	Experts are sounding an alarm.
sprachlos	speechless

A5

kommunizieren	to communicate
das **Internet**	Internet
das **Internet-Café**, -Cafés	Internet cafe
aufschreiben	to write down
Schreiben Sie ein paar Tipps auf.	Write down a few tips.
die **Nachbarin**, Nachbarinnen	neighbor
vh(s) (= Volkshochschule)	adult evening school
anklicken	to click (on)
das **Kino-Pogramm**, -Programme	film program
der **Biergarten**, -gärten	beer garden
aneinander vorbei	past each other
aneinander vorbei sprechen	to talk past each other
faxen	to fax
einander	each other
die **E-mail**, E-mails (engl.)	E-mail

A6

neulich	recently
gemütlich	snug, cozy
Neulich sitzen wir gemütlich im Café.	Recently we were sitting cozily in a cafe.
obwohl	although
das **Handy**, Handys	cellular phone
die **Handtasche**, -taschen	handbag

A7

das **Kommunikationsmedium**, -medien	means of communication

3 Im Fernsehen: 8. Juni

A8

das **Medien-Ereignis**, -Ereignisse	media event
analysieren	analyze
die **Kennzeichnung**	labeling
die **Gen-Lebensmittel** (Pl.)	genetically engineered foods
die **Tagesschau**	news of the day (television)
die **Gute-Nacht-Geschichte**, -Geschichten	bedtime story
Samschtig (schweiz. = Samstag)	(Swiss) Saturday
der **Jass** (= schweizerisches Kartenspiel)	jass, a Swiss card game
das **Zahlenlotto**	lottery in which participants try to guess the correct numbers
das **Meteo** (schweiz. = Wetterbericht)	(Swiss) weather report
das **Wort zum Sonntag**	"Word for Sunday" (short religious broadcast)
der/die **Behinderte**, die Behinderten	handicapped
der **Behindertensport**	sports for the handicapped
derfür (schweiz. = dafür)	for
derwider (schweiz. = dagegen)	against
das **Bühnenstück**, -stücke	stage play
die **Feier**, Feiern	celebration, ceremony
die **Eröffnungsfeier**, -feiern	opening ceremony
das **Eröffnungsspiel**	opening game, first game
das **Rad** (= das Fahrrad)	bicycle
Rad (= Radsport)	cycling
der/das **Final** (schweiz. = das Finale)	finale
das **Reiten**	riding, equestrian events
der **Thriller**, Thriller	thriller

die **Europameisterschaft**, -meisterschaften (= EM)	European Championship
die **Sportschau**	sports news (TV)
das **Boxen**	boxing
der **Kampf**, Kämpfe	fight
die **Singles** (Pl.)	singles
der/die **Mitwirkende**, die Mitwirkenden	participants, performers
die **Familiensaga**, -sagas	family saga
die **Komödie**, Komödien	comedy
die **Krimikomödie**, -komödien	crime comedy
das **Journal**, Journale	journal, magazine
das **Studio**, Studios	studio
das aktuelle Sport-Studio	"The Latest in Sports" (a Saturday-night TV institution)
das **Resultat**, Resultate	result
die **Verdammnis**	damnation
der **Chaot**, Chaoten	chaotic person
die **Chaoten-Show**, -Shows	"Chaotic People Show"
die **Serie**, Serien	series
der **Actionfilm**, -filme	action film
die **Zeichenerklärung**, -erklärungen	legend, explanation of symbols
schwarzweiß	black-and-white
der **Zweikanalton**	dual-channel sound
der **Stereoton**	stereophonic sound
die **Erleichterung**	relief, aid, help
der **Samstagskrimi**, -krimis	Saturday crime show
ausgetrickst	tricked
Erleichterung für Hörbehinderte	help for the hard of hearing
die **Meldung**, Meldungen	announcement, news
der **Beitrag**, Beiträge	contribution, report
laufen	to run, to be shown
die Sendung läuft im Programm...	the broadcast is being shown on Channel...

A9

der **Ausschnitt**, Ausschnitte	excerpt
die **Fußball-Europa-meisterschaft** (= EM)	European Football Championship
heißen	to be reported, to be said
im Bericht heißt es, dass...	in the report they say...
melden	to announce, report
In der Tagesschau wird gemeldet, dass...	In the news on TV they report that...

4 In der Tageszeitung: 9. Juni

die **Tageszeitung**, -zeitungen	daily newspaper

A10

die **Fernsehnachrichten** (Pl.)	TV news
das **Inland**	at home, national (here in the context of news)
die **Partei**, Parteien	party
der **Parteitag**, Parteitage	party conference, convention
die **FDP** (Freie Demo-kratische Partei)	Free Democratic Party
geben, sich	to give oneself
Die FDP gibt sich ein neues Programm.	The FDP gives itself a new program.
attackieren	to attack
weltweit	worldwide
der **Protest**, Proteste	protest
chinesisch	Chinese
der **Atomtest**, Atomtests	atomic tests
weltweite Proteste gegen chinesische Atomtests	worldwide protests against Chinese atomic tests
der **Blitz**, Blitze	lightning
Blitz tötet Mann in Hamburg	Lightning kills man in Hamburg
trotz	despite
die **Bewölkung**	clouds
Trotz leichter Bewölkung im Süden meist sonnig.	Mostly sunny in the South despite light clouds.
höchst-	highest, maximum
die **Höchsttemperatur**, -temperaturen	maximum temperature
die **Aussicht**, Aussichten	outlook
das **Toto**	football pools
die **Superzahl**	extra-lucky number
eröffnet	opened
farbenfroh	colorful
das **Spektakel**	spectacle
das **Stadion**, Stadien	stadium
rund	approximately
rund 400 Millionen Fußball-fans	approximately 400 million football fans
die **Halbzeit**, -zeiten	half(time)
in der ersten Halbzeit	in the first half
schießen	to shoot
das 1:0 schießen	to shoot the 1-to-0 goal
das **Handspiel**	illegal use of the hands
der **Strafraum**	penalty area
der **Elfmeter**, Elfmeter	penalty kick
ausgleichen	to tie, to even the score
verdienen	to earn, to deserve
der **Punkt**, Punkte	point
die **Leistung**, Leistungen	achievement, performance
Die Schweizer verdienen den Punkt wegen ihrer guten Leistung.	The Swiss deserve the point because of their good performance.
der **Rand**, Ränder	fringe, edge

am Rande der Eröffnungs-feier	on the fringes of the opening ceremony
festnehmen	to arrest
randalieren	to rampage
die **Störung**, Störungen	disturbance
der **Start**, Starts	start
das **Tor**, Tore	goal
das **Elfmeter-Tor**, -Tore	goal from the penalty kick
jubeln	to exult, to be jubilant
das **Lokale**	local news
Mecklenburg-Vorpommern	Mecklenburg – Western Pomerania
das **Bundesland**, -länder	federal state
das **Backverbot**	baking prohibition
aufheben	to abolish
Mecklenburg-Vorpommern hat das Backverbot am Sonntag aufgehoben.	Mecklenburg – Western Pomerania has abolished the Sunday-baking prohibition.
weiterhin	still, as before
touristisch	tourist (adj.)
erlauben	to allow, to permit
der **Konsum**	consumption, consumer affairs
der **Appell**, Appelle	appeal
der **Ärztetag**	physicians' convention
der 99. Deutsche Ärztetag	99th Physicians' Convention
Köln	Cologne
gentechnisch	genetically engineered
verändert	changed, altered
verlangen	to demand
die Kennzeichnung von gentechnisch veränderten Lebensmitteln verlangen	to demand the labeling of genetically altered foods
das **Risiko**, Risiken	risk
menschlich	human
ein Risiko für die mensch-liche Gesundheit	a risk for the health of human beings
die **Pflicht**, Pflichten	duty, obligation
die **Kennzeichnungs-pflicht**	labeling requirement
vorsichtig	cautious, careful
die **Formulierung**, Formulierungen	formulation
die **Auseinandersetzung**, Auseinandersetzungen	confrontation
die **Kommission**, Kommissionen	commission
die **EU** (= Europäische Union)	European Union
die **EU**-Kommission	E.U. Commission

5 Aussprache

A12

momentan	momentary, respective
der **Einer**, Einer	the "one" (one to nine)
der **Zehner**, Zehner	the (multiples of) "ten"

A13

die **Jahreszahl**, Jahreszahlen	year
die **Radiosendung**, -sendungen	radio broadcast
der **Farbfilm**, Farbfilme	color film

6 Wortschatz

A14

das **Medien-Produkt**, -produkte	media product
Werbeslogan, -slogans	advertising slogan
nachschlagen	to look up
Schlagen Sie im Wörterbuch nach.	Look it up in the dictio-nary.
die **Technik**, Techniken	technology
technisch	technical
original	original
der **Gewinn**, Gewinne	profit
entscheiden	to decide

A16

täglich	daily, every day
läuten	to ring
Der Wecker läutet.	The alarm clock rings.
einschalten (sich)	to go on, to turn itself on
der **Radiowecker**, -wecker	radio alarm clock
der **Sender**, Sender	station
der **Lieblingssender**, -sender	favorite station
das **TV** (= Television, Fernsehen)	television
das **Frühstücks-TV**	breakfast TV
der **Kiosk**, Kioske	kiosk
die **Haltestelle**, Haltestellen	stop (for a bus, streetcar etc.)
durchblättern	to leaf through
der **Schreibtisch**, -tische	desk
der **Anrufbeantworter**, -beantworter	answering machine
zurückrufen	to call back
die **Mail-Box**, -Boxen (engl.)	mailbox
schicken	to send
die **Post**	mail
die **Kantine**, Kantinen	canteen
die **Wochenzeitschrift**, -zeitschriften	weekly magazine
hereinschauen	to look in

der **Plattenladen**, -läden	record store
der **Player**, Player	(CD) player

A18

der **Sprachunterricht**	language instruction
die **Kursstunde**	course hour

7 Grammatik

kaus**al**	causal
konzess**iv**	concessive
verm**issen**	to miss
surfen	to surf
im Internet surfen	to surf in the Internet
geschr**ieben**	written
geschriebene Sprache	written language
gespr**ochen**	spoken
der **Gegengrund**	argument against, reason to the contrary

die **Folgerung**, Folgerungen	conclusion, consequence, result
superschnell	super-fast
das **Adverb**, Adverbien	adverb
deswegen	for that reason, therefore
die **Voraussetzung**, Voraussetzungen	premise, requirement, condition
unerwartet	unexpected
unerwartete Folgerung	unexpected result
die **Verwendung**, Verwendungen	use
obgleich	although
das **Verbindungsadverb**, -adverbien	linking adverb, conjunct
reziprok	reciprocal
reziproke Verben	reciprocal verb
begegnen	to meet

23 Zwischenstopp „Grundbaustein"

der **Zwischenstopp**, Zwischenstopps	stopover
der **Grundbaustein**	basic knowledge

1 „Grundbaustein" – was ist das?

A1

das **Zertifikat**, Zertifikate	certificate
Deutsch als Fremdsprache	German as a foreign language
das **Niveau**, Niveaus	level
die **Prüfung**, Prüfungen	test
bestätigen	to confirm
die **Alltagssituation**, -situationen	everyday situation
bewältigen	to cope with, to manage
bearbeiten	to work on/through
der **Tscheche**, Tschechen	Czech
der **Kongress**, Kongresse	conference
die **Physik**	physics
die **Umweltphysik**	environmental physics
die **Studienkollegin**, -kolleginnen	fellow student

2 Milan und Andrea

A3

das **Programmangebot**, -angebote	program offering

das **Kulturprogramm**, -programme	cultural program
die **Agenda** (schweiz.)	happenings, events
das **Polaroid**, Polaroids	Polaroid
manipulieren	to manipulate
faszinieren	to fascinate
das **Werk**, Werke	work (of art, literature etc.)
die **Galerie**, Galerien	gallery
die **Kulturwerkstatt**, -werkstätten	cultural workshop
vielfältig	diverse
ein vielfältiges Programm anbieten	to offer a diverse program
der **Zirkus**, Zirkusse	circus
kulinarisch	culinary
die **Mischung**, Mischungen	mixture
kühl	cool
die **Winternacht**, -nächte	winter night
die **Abendmusik**	evening church concert
Armenien	Armenia
die **Herkunft**	origin, ancestry
das **Orgelkonzert**, -konzerte	organ concert
der **Ausdruck**	expression
zum Ausdruck kommen	to find expression
französisch	French
der **Komponist**, Komponisten	composer
spirituell	spiritual, religious
armenisch	Armenian
der **HipHop**	hip hop
überraschen	to surprise

der **Hit**, Hits	hit
live (engl.)	live
besingen	to sing about

A4

der **Hbf.**/der **HB**	main train station
(= der Hauptbahnhof)	
der **IR** (= der Interregiozug)	"Interregio" express train
die **SBB** (Pl.) (= Schweize-	Swiss Federal Railway
rische Bundesbahnen)	

A5

erfragen	to ask for and obtain
reserviert	reserved
der reservierte Platz	reserved seat
der **Großraumwagen**,	open car (not divided into
-wagen/-wägen	compartments)
der **Raucher**, Raucher	smoking car, smoker
gratis	free of charge

A6

das **Tennis**	tennis
gewinnen	to win
Wer hat im Tennis	Who won in tennis?
gewonnen?	
die **Vorhersage**,	forecast
-vorhersagen	
die **Wettervorhersage**,	weather forecast
-vorhersagen	
Süddeutschland	South Germany
vormittags	morning, forenoon
das **Flusstal**, -täler	river valley
der **Nebel**, Nebel	fog
minus (-)	minus (-)
plus (+)	plus (+)
zwischen –2 und +5 Grad	between –2° C and + 5° C
	(+28.4° F and +41° F)
das **Reiseland**, -länder	tourist country, vacation
	destination
die **Alpen** (Pl.)	the Alps
die **Westalpen** (Pl.)	the Western Alps
der **Schneefall**, -fälle	snowfall
In den Westalpen stark	In the Western Alps heavy
bewölkt und Schneefall.	clouds and snowfall.
anfangs	at first, in the morning
vermehrt	increased
Im Laufe des Sonntags	In the course of Sunday
vermehrt Sonne.	increased sunshine.
neblig	foggy
der **Gesundheitstipp**,	health tip
-tipps	
die **Erkältung**, Erkältungen	cold
triumphal	triumphant
der **Sieg**, Siege	victory
die **Tennis-Szene**	tennis scene
der **Star**, Stars	star

bisher	up to now
die **Gewinnerin**,	winner
Gewinnerinnen	
das **Turnier**, Turniere	tournament
die **Dame**, Damen	lady
das **Damen-Finale**	women's finals
der **Erfolg**, Erfolge	success, victory
demonstrieren	to demonstrate, to show
bereits	already
die **Tennis-Welt**	the tennis world
das **Talent**, Talente	talent
das **Doppel**	doubles
die **Weißrussin**,	White Russian
-russinnen	
der **Triumph**, Triumphe	triumph
unterstützen	to support
das **Racket**, Rackets	racket
drücken	to press
Sie drückte mir ein Racket	She pressed a racket into
in die Hand.	my hand.
das **Damen-Tennis**	women's tennis
ablösen	to replace, to take over
	from
der **Amerikaner**,	American
Amerikaner	
der **Spanier**, Spanier	Spaniard
die **Rangliste**, -listen	rankings
die **Weltrangliste**	world rankings
der **Satz**, Sätze	set
in drei Sätzen 6:2, 6:3	in three sets: 6 to 2,
und 6:3	6 to 3, and 6 to 3

A7

herstellen	to establish
Kontakt herstellen	to establish contact
der/die **Reisende**,	traveler
die Reisenden	
das **Reiseziel**, -ziele	destination

A8

die **Durchsage**,	announcement
Durchsagen	

A9

die **Bilderserie**, -serien	series of pictures

3 Sprachenbiografie

die **Sprachenbiografie**,	language-learning
-biografien	biography

A10

der **Kindergarten**, -gärten	kindergarten
die **Schulzeit**	schooldays
Latein	Latin
dank	thanks to

Französisch dank Freunden
der **Aufenthalt**,
  Aufenthalte
French thanks to friends
sojourn, stay, period of
  living

der **Auslandsaufenthalt**,
  -aufenthalte
stay abroad, period of
  living abroad

die **Bemerkung**,
  Bemerkungen
remark

Russisch
Russian

das **Wirtschaftsdeutsch**
economic German

das **Diplom**, Diplome
diploma

die **Wunschsprache**,
  Wunschsprachen
desired language, lan-
  guage one wishes to
  learn

A12

das **Sprachdiplom**,
  -diplome
language diploma

das **Sprachtraining**
language training

die **Intensivgruppe**,
  -gruppen
intensive groups

wirtschaftlich
economical

der **Spracherfolg**
language success

mein wirtschaftlicher Weg
  zum Spracherfolg
my economical way to
  language success

die **Effizienz**
efficiency

der **Lernpartner**,
  -partner
learning partner

der **Tageskurs**, -kurse
day course

der **Abendkurs**, -kurse
evening course

der **Samstagskurs**,
  -kurse
Saturday course

der **Ferienkurs**, -kurse
vacation course

die **Nachhilfe**,
  Nachhilfen
private tutoring,
  private lessons

die **Schülernachhilfe**
private tutoring for pupils
  still in school

extern
external

die **Fachsprache**,
  Fachsprachen
technical language,
  specialized language

die **Kompetenz**
competence

das **Sprachinstitut**,
  -institute
language institute, lan-
  guage school

der **Treffpunkt**, -punkte
meeting place

24 Fremd(e)

die **Fremde**
foreign land, foreign
  country

der/die **Fremde**,
  die Fremden
stranger, foreigner

1 Gastarbeiter

der **Arbeiter**, Arbeiter
worker

der **Gastarbeiter**,
  -arbeiter
guest worker

A2

die **Definition**, Definitionen
definition

zurückkehren
to go back

türkisch
Turkish

die türkischen Gastarbeiter
Turkish guest workers

der **Schnurrbart**, -bärte
moustache

gebückt
bent

mit gebücktem Rücken
with bent back

die **Arbeiterin**,
  Arbeiterinnen
worker

A3

deutschsprachig
German-speaking

die deutschsprachigen
  Länder
German-speaking
  countries

die **Wirtschaft**
economy

die **Arbeitskräfte** (Pl.)
workers

Die Wirtschaft brauchte
  dringend neue Arbeits-
  kräfte.
The economy urgently
  needed new workers.

anwerben
to recruit

der **Italiener**, Italiener
Italian

der **Portugiese**,
  Portugiesen
Spaniard
Portuguese

der **Türke**, Türken
Turk

der **Jugoslawe**,
  Jugoslawen
Yugoslavian

der **Grieche**, Griechen
Greek

aufmachen, sich
to set out

Mitteleuropa
Central Europe

Hunderttausende machten
  sich auf nach Mittel-
  europa.
Hundreds of thousands set
  out for Central Europe.

gespart
saved

das gesparte Geld
saved money, savings

A4

zeitlich
chronological

einordnen
to arrange, to order

Aussagen zeitlich einordnen
to order statements
  chronologically

der **Zeit-Pfeil**, -Pfeile
time-arrow

ununterbrochen
uninterrupted

sogenannt
so-called

das **Gastland**, Gastländer
host country

in den sogenannten
  Gastländern arbeiten
to work in the so-called
  host countries

sobald
as soon as

gelingen
to succeed, to manage

nachkommen	to follow
der/die **Verwandte**, die Verwandten	relative
der **Urlaub**	holiday, vacation
nur vom Urlaub kennen	to know only from vacations

A5

verändern	to change
zweideutig	ambivalent
alles ist so zweideutig	everything is so ambivalent
die **Zunge**	tongue
nachdem	after
solange	as long as
zurückkehren	to go back, to return
bevor	before

2 Integration

die **Integration**	integration

A7

der **Begriff**, Begriffe	concept, term
bezeichnen	to describe as, to call
ausschließen	to exclude
Bosnien	Bosnia
gemischt	mixed
die **Ehe**, Ehen	marriage
als Kind aus einer gemischten Ehe	the child of a mixed marriage
die **Flucht**	escape, flight
schwierig	difficult
die **Behörde**, Behörden	bureau, board
die **Schulbehörde**, -behörden	school board
die **Beraterin**, Beraterinnen	adviser
ausländisch	foreign
die Integration von ausländischen Kindern	the integration of foreign children
das **Missverständnis**, Missverständnisse	misunderstanding
die **Intoleranz**	intolerance
unheimlich	extremely
unheimlich schwer	extremely difficult
betroffen (betreffen)	concerned
ein Gespräch zwischen betroffenen Personen herstellen	to arrange a conversation between the persons concerned

A8

gelungen (gelingen)	successful (to succeed)
die **Jugendarbeit**	youth-work
gelungene Jugendarbeit	successful youth-work
das **Festival**, Festivals	festival

vergangen	past, last
am vergangenen Wochenende	this past weekend, last weekend
sehenswert	worth seeing
die **Aufführung**, Aufführungen	performance
die **Tanz-Gruppe**, -Gruppen	dance troupe
der **Zuschauer**, Zuschauer	spectator, member of an audience
das **Jugendzentrum**, -zentren	youth center
der **Workshop**, Workshops	workshop
der **Tanz-Workshop**, -Workshops	dance workshop
seither	since then
wöchentlich	weekly, per week
der **Trainer**, Trainer	trainer
der **Betreuer**, Betreuer	social worker, supervisor
proben	to rehearse
die **Streetdance-Gruppe**, -Gruppen	street-dance troupe
außergewöhnlich	extraordinary
der **Aspekt**, Aspekte	aspect

3 „Fremd im eigenen Land"

A10

die **Hoffnung**, Hoffnungen	hope
golden	golden
der **Adler**, Adler	eagle
drauf (= darauf)	on it
bedingen	to cause
raufen	to pull, to tear
Dies bedingt, dass ich mir oft die Haare rauf.	This often causes me to tear my hair.
der **Ärger**	anger
zu **Hauf**	heaps of
niemals	never
saufen	to drink (alcohol) in large quantities
das **Gerede**	talk, chatter
der **Zusammenschluss**	joining together, union
ausweisen, sich	to show one's papers, to establish one's identity
beweisen	to prove
Identität beweisen	to prove one's identity
ungewöhnlich	unusual
der **Afro-Deutsche**, die -Deutschen	Afro-German
das **System**, Systeme	system
gestatten	to allow, to permit
Gestatten Sie, mein Name ist . . .	Permit me – my name is . . .
ansehen	to look at, to see

jemandem etwas ansehen	to see that someone is or has something
der **Aussiedler**, Aussiedler	resettled person
der **Immigrant**, Immigranten	immigrant
der **Staatsbürger**, Staatsbürger	citizen of a country
zufällig	by chance, by accident
anerkannt	acknowledged, accepted, officially recognized

A11

zusammenbringen	to bring together
ursprünglich	originally, at first
von klein auf	since we were little
das **Gemeinsame**	what one has in common with others
der **Außenseiter**, Außenseiter	outsider
korrekt	correct
politisch korrekt	politically correct
der **Rassismus**	racism
kämpfen	to fight
gegen Rassismus und Vorurteile kämpfen	to fight against racism and prejudice
das **Image**	image
kulturell	cultural
die **Rasse**, Rassen	race
der **Blödsinn**	nonsense
So ein Blödsinn!	What a load of nonsense!
die **Klasse**, Klassen	class
die soziale Klasse	social class, social stratum

4 Aussprache

A12

die **Akzentgruppe**, -gruppen	accent group
mitklopfen	to knock along in time, to beat time
gliedern	to arrange, to divide

A13

klatschen	to clap
selbstverständlich	naturally, of course
die **Überstunde**, -stunden	overtime
das **Arbeitsklima**	working atmosphere
das **Vergnügen**	pleasure

A14

| die **Kritik**, Kritiken | criticism, critique |

5 Wortschatz

A15

der **Buchstabe**, Buchstaben	letter
der **Ast**, Äste	bough
sagen, sich	to say to oneself
er sagte sich, …	he said to himself …
der **Garten**, Gärten	garden

A17

das **Industrieland**, -länder	industrial nation
auswandern	to emigrate
einwandern	to immigrate
anpassen, sich	to adapt (oneself)

6 Grammatik

die **Jüngeren** (Pl.)	younger people
das **Plusquamperfekt**	past perfect
nicht-gleichzeitig	non-simultaneous
hierher	here, to this place
zurückgehen	to go back
temporal	temporal, time
ehe	before
seitdem	since
logisch	logical
ein logischer Kontrast	a logical contrast
das **Heimweh**	homesickness
die **Probe**, Proben	rehearsal
danach	afterward

25 Familie, Freunde, Feste

1 Familie Weber: drei Generationen

A1

vor allem	above all
die **Selbstverständlichkeit**	matter of course, self-evident fact
die **Rolle**, Rollen	role
eine zentrale Rolle spielen	to play a central role
der/die **Große**, die Großen	grown-up children
der **Ehepartner**, -partner	spouse

A2

die **Arbeitsteilung**	division of labor, allocation of work
die **Hausaufgabe**, -aufgaben	household chore, housework
das **Kaninchen**, Kaninchen	rabbit
der **Geburtsvorbereitungskurs**, -kurse	birth preparation course

der/die **Kleine**, die Kleinen	little child, little one	die wichtigen Entscheidun-	to make the most impor-
wickeln	to change diapers	gen treffen	tant decisions
füttern	to feed	**sauber machen**	to clean
kümmern, sich	to take care of, to look	die **Karriere**, Karrieren	career
	after	die **Ausnahme**,	exception
schreien	to cry	Ausnahmen	
teilen, sich	to divide, to share	Das war die große	That was the great excep-
die **Hausarbeit**, -arbeiten	household chore,	Ausnahme.	tion.
	housework	**ausüben**	to practice, to carry on
zuständig	in charge, responsible	einen Beruf ausüben	to work, to have a job, to
zuständig sein für	to be in charge of, to be		work at a job or career
	responsible for	**heutzutage**	nowadays
		aushandeln	to negotiate

A3

ordentlich	orderly
Unsere Kinder könnten	Our children could be
ordentlicher sein.	a little more orderly.

A6

das **Rollenverhalten**	role behavior
üblich	usual, normal
der **Familienvater**,	husband and father,
-väter	head of the family
die **Hausfrau**, -frauen	housewife
verantwortlich	responsible

2 Lebensformen – früher und heute

die **Lebensform**, -formen	way of life

A4

das **Modell**, Modelle	model
das **Familien-Modell**,	family model
-Modelle	
jemand in Bewegung	to keep someone in
halten	motion, to keep some-
	one active
beruflich	working, professional
aktiv	active, busy
berufstätig	working
erziehen	to raise, to bring up
allein erziehende Mutter	single mother
der **Streit**	fight, quarrel
es gibt Streit über …	there is a fight about …
die **Großfamilie**, -familien	extended family
allerdings	of course

A5

die **Schrumpf-Familie**,	"shrunken" or reduced
-Familien	family
das **Drittel**, Drittel	third
zu **zweit**	together with someone,
	as a couple
zunehmen	to increase
ständig	constant
die **Männerrolle**, -rollen	male role
die **Frauenrolle**, -rollen	female role
Männer- und Frauenrollen	male and female roles
praktisch	practically
praktisch jeder Mann	practically every man
die **Autorität**,	authority
Autoritäten	
treffen	to make (in the context of
	decisions)

3 Freunde – die bessere Familie?

A7

trösten	to comfort, to console
schimpfen	to scold
beschützen	to protect
ewig	eternal
dankbar	grateful
ewig dankbar sein müssen	to have to be eternally
	grateful
vertraut	familiar, intimate, close
konkurrieren	to compete
denn	than
je	ever
Freunde sind heute nötiger	Today friends are more
denn je.	necessary than ever.
verlassen, sich	to count on, to rely on
Auf die Familie kann man	You can no longer rely on
sich nicht mehr allein	your family alone.
verlassen.	
einengen	to hem in
Nähe, ohne eingeengt zu	closeness without being
werden	hemmed in
die **Freundschaft**,	friendship
Freundschaften	
kündigen	to terminate
lebenslang	lifelong

A8

eintönig	monotonous
dahinfliegen	to fly (as in "Time flies.")
die **Menge**, Mengen	quantity, amount, number
das **Dia**, Dias	slide
jede Menge Dias	tons and tons of slides

kalt stellen	to chill, to put in the refridgerator
Stell schon mal das Bier kalt!	You can already put the beer in the fridge!
der **Anruf**, Anrufe	phone call
wegfahren	to go away, to go on a trip

A9

die **Blume**, Blumen	flower
gießen	to water
die Blumen gießen	to water the flowers

A10

all	all
all diese Freunde	all these friends

4 Weihnachten – ein Familienfest?

das **Familienfest**, -feste	family celebration, family gathering

A11

zusammenkommen	to come together
das **Kaffeetrinken**	afternoon coffee, coffee klatsch
der **Weihnachtsbaum**, -bäume	Christmas tree
die **Bescherung**, Bescherungen	gift-giving
das **Geschenk**, Geschenke	gift
der **Gottesdienst**, Gottesdienste	church service
der **Zweig**, -Zweige	branch
der **Tannenzweig**, -zweige	fir branch
die **Kerze**, Kerzen	candle
die **Nuss**, Nüsse	nut
selbst gebastelt	homemade
dekorieren	to decorate
weihnachtlich	Christmassy
der **Zimtstern**, -sterne	cinnamon star (cookie)
zusammensitzen	to sit together
die **Süßigkeit**, Süßigkeiten	sweet

A13

der **Zeitungsartikel**, -artikel	newspaper article
die **Äußerung**, Äußerungen	statement
beliebt	popular
kommerziell	commercial
unfeierlich	unfestive
nervig	nerve-racking
die **Weihnachtszeit**	Christmastime
fleißig	busy, industrious, eager
Trotzdem machen alle fleißig mit.	Still, everyone eagerly goes along with it.

erwarten	to expect
das **Zusammensein**	being together
ausschlafen	to sleep in
die **Enttäuschung**, Enttäuschungen	disappointment
vorprogrammieren	to pre-program, to program in advance
Enttäuschungen sind damit schon vorprogrammiert.	With that, disappointments are already programmed in advance.
ausgestorben	dead, lifeless, deserted
Die Straßen sind wie ausgestorben.	The streets are deserted.
total	total, absolute
die totale Ruhe genießen	to enjoy absolute quiet

A14

der **Brauch**, Bräuche	custom
Bei uns ist es ein Brauch, . . .	We have the custom of/that . . .

5 Frohe Ostern!

Ostern	Easter

A15

die **Tradition**, Traditionen	tradition
ausblasen	to blow (eggs)
bemalen	to paint
die **Eierschale**, Eierschalen	eggshell
die **Vase**, Vasen	vase
der **Ostersonntag**	Easter Sunday
die **Schlüsselblume**, Schlüsselblumen	cowslip
das **Vergissmeinnicht**	forget-me-not
füllen	to fill
das **Osterei**, Ostereier	Easter egg
versteckt	hidden
Überall waren Ostereier versteckt.	Easter eggs were hidden everywhere.
die **Couch**	couch
das **Bücherregal**, -regale	bookshelf
der **Vorhang**, Vorhänge	curtain
der **Marzipan**	marzipan
die **Christenheit**	Christendom
die **Auferstehung**	resurrection
die **Osterzeit**	Eastertime
der **Karsamstag**	Holy Saturday
der **Vollmond**	full moon
das **Frühjahr**	spring
der **Frühjahrsvollmond**	spring moon
der **Frühlingsanfang**	beginning of spring

A16

der **Volkskundler**, Volkskundler	folklorist, folklore scholar

der **Ursprung**, Ursprünge	origin
das **Brauchtum**	custom
das **Osterfest**	(celebration of) Easter
das **Pessach-Fest**	Pesach, Passover
das **Frühlingsfest**, -feste	spring festival
das **Lamm**, Lämmer	lamb
opfern	to sacrifice
die **Juden** (Pl.)	the Jews
der **Auszug**	procession, departure, exodus
Ägypten	Egypt
der Auszug der Juden aus Ägypten	the Exodus of the Jews from Egypt
die **Christen** (Pl.)	the Christians
die **Befreiung**	liberation
die **Sünde**, Sünden	sin
der **Hase**, Hasen	hare
die **Fruchtbarkeit**	fertility
das **Osterbrot**	Easter bread
verschenken	to give
die **Henne**, Hennen	hen
der **Osterhase**	Easter bunny
religiös	religious
die religiöse Bedeutung verlieren	to lose the religious meaning
ausruhen, sich	to rest, to relax

6 Aussprache

A18
senden	to send, to extend
die besten Grüße senden	to extend the fondest regards
demnächst	soon
das **Neujahr**	New Year
Kommt uns zu Neujahr besuchen.	Come visit us over New Year's.

A19
| der **Verstärker**, Verstärker | intensifier |

intensiv	intense, strong
der **Sprecher**, Sprecher	speaker
die **Intensität**	intensity

7 Wortschatz

A20
der **Glückwunsch**, Glückwünsche	congratulations
der **Anlass**, Anlässe	occasion
Viel Glück!	Good luck!
die **Hochzeit**, Hochzeiten	wedding
der **Geburtstag**, -tage	birthday
die **Gratulation**, Gratulationen	congratulations

A21
der **Kartengruß**, -grüße	greetings in a card
wörtlich	verbatim, word for word
Notieren Sie wörtlich.	Note down word for word.

8 Grammatik

längst	long since
der/die **Unbekannte**, die Unbekannten	unknown person, person with whom one is not acquainted
die **Adjektiv-Endung**, -Endungen	adjectival ending
die **Genitiv-Umschreibung**	genitive paraphrase
die **Erziehung**	education, upbringing
die **Kindererziehung**	bringing up children, raising children
angehen	to concern
Kindererziehung geht beide Partner an.	Raising children concerns both partners.
die **Verantwortung**	responsibility
beitragen	to contribute
das **Computerspiel**, -spiele	computer game

26 Schule und Ausbildung

1 Schulerfahrungen

| die **Schulerfahrung**, -erfahrungen | school experience |

A1
das **Fach**, Fächer	subject
das **Schulfach**, Schulfächer	school subject
die **Note**, Noten	grade, mark
der **Stundenplan**, -pläne	daily schedule

die **Mathematik**	mathematics
die **Geschichte**	history
die **Informatik**	computer science
die **Kunst**	art
die **Sozialkunde**	social studies
die **Chemie**	chemistry
die **Biologie**	biology
das **Schuljahr**, -jahre	school year
das **Halbjahr**, -jahre	semester

die **Benotung**	grading, marking
die **Religionslehre**	religious instruction, religion class
die **Heimatkunde**	a subject embracing local history, culture, and geography
die **Erdkunde** (= Geographie)	geography
die **Naturkunde** (= Biologie)	biology

A2

| das **Lieblingsfach**, -fächer | favorite subject |

A3

die **Schulerinnerungen** (Pl.)	memories of school
auswendig	by heart
Gedichte auswendig lernen	to learn poems by heart
die **Stunde**, Stunden	hour of instruction
das **Klo**, Klos (= WC)	lavatory
die **Aufregung**	excitement
vor Aufregung nicht sprechen können	to be too excited to speak
der **Lieblingslehrer**, -lehrer	favorite teacher
die **Lieblingslehrerin**, -lehrerinnen	favorite teacher
die **Klassenarbeit**, -arbeiten	classwork

2 Für das Leben lernen wir ...

A4

versagen	to fail
Die Schule hat völlig versagt.	Schools have failed completely.
unnötig	unnecessary
der **Kram**	stuff
vollstopfen	to cram full
sich den Kopf mit unnötigem Kram vollstopfen	to cram one's head full of useless stuff
die **Kooperation**	cooperation
die **Flexibilität**	flexibility
der **Unternehmer**, Unternehmer	entrepreneur
heben	to raise
den Finger heben	to raise one's finger
aufbekommen	to be assigned, to be given
Hausaufgaben aufbekommen	to be given homework assignments
eingehen	to be responsive (to someone's needs etc.)
Die Lehrer versuchen, auf die Schüler einzugehen.	The teachers try to be responsive to the pupils' needs.
sogar	even

| die **Bankkauffrau**, -frauen | qualified bank clerk |
| die **Rechtschreibung** | spelling, orthography |

A5

das **Unterrichtsziel**, -ziele	teaching aims
die **Gymnasiallehrerin**, -lehrerinnen	college-preparatory high-school teacher
die **Gesamtschule**, -schulen	comprehensive school (academic and general)
vertreten	to represent, to give, to express
Die Schüler können ihre Meinung vertreten.	The pupils can express their opinion.
der **Fremdsprachenunterricht**	foreign language instruction
die **Bedeutung**	importance
von großer Bedeutung sein	to be of great importance
selbständig (= selbstständig)	independent

3 Der Weg in den Beruf

A7

der **Betrieb**, Betriebe	firm, company
das **Betriebsklima**	atmosphere at work
die **Berufsausbildung**, -ausbildungen	vocational training
der **Fahrzeugbauer**, -bauer	automobile constructor, licensed auto worker
die **Werkstatt**, Werkstätten	workshop
die **Autowerkstatt**, -werkstätten	automobile workshop
insgesamt	in all
die **Reparatur**, Reparaturen	repair
übernehmen	to take over
Arbeiten übernehmen	to take over jobs, to take over tasks
das **Lehrjahr**, Lehrjahre	apprenticeship year
die **Berufsschule**, -schulen	vocational school
die **Zwischenprüfung**, -prüfungen	intermediate examination
bestehen	to pass
die Zwischenprüfung bestehen	to pass the intermediate examination
theoretisch	theoretical
die **Abschlussprüfung**, -prüfungen	final examination
ablegen	to take, to pass
die theoretische und praktische Abschlussprüfung ablegen	to pass the theoretical and practical final examination
der **Geselle**, Gesellen	journeyman

weiterlernen	to continue to learn
der **Techniker**, Techniker	technician
der **Flugzeugtechniker**, -techniker	aircraft technician
der **Pilot**, Piloten	pilot

A8

der **Lehrherr**, -herren	master (of an apprentice)
der **Dorn**, Dornen	thorn
Sein Gesicht war mir ein Dorn im Auge.	His face was a thorn in my side.
der **Ernst**	seriousness
Der Ernst des Lebens beginnt.	The seriousness of life begins.
pfeifen	to whistle
loben	to praise
peinlich	embarrassing
insgeheim	secretly, to oneself
zurechtfinden, sich	to find one's way around, to get used to things
hinauf	up
die **Direktion**, Direktionen	manager's office
anmelden (sich)	to register, to enroll
kräftig	powerful
dunkelbraun	dark brown
funkeln	to sparkle
mit funkelnden Augen	with eyes that sparkled
anbrüllen	to shout at, to roar at
der **Augenblick**, -blicke	moment
die **Schattseite** (= Schattenseite)	shady side, dark side
der **Roman**, Romane	novel
alarmieren	to alarm
alarmierend	alarming
alarmierende Zahlen für die Jugendlichen	alarming statistics for young people
die **Lehrstelle**, -stellen	apprenticeship
nordrhein-westfälisch	North Rhine - Westphalian
der **Lehrling**, Lehrlinge	apprentice
der **Schreinerlehrling**, -lehrlinge	cabinet maker's apprentice
der **Vertreter**, Vertreter	representative, member
der **Handel**	commerce
Vertreter von Handel und Industrie	members of commerce and industry
der **Bauarbeiter**, -arbeiter	construction worker
der **Koch**, Köche	cook
kaufmännisch	business, commercial
kaufmännische Berufe	commercial professions
warnen	to warn
weiterführen	to continue
weiterführende Schulen	schools that go beyond minimum compulsory education
honorieren	to honor, to respect

die **Praxis**	practice, practical experience
Die Betriebe honorieren Praxis und Erfahrung.	The companies respect practical knowledge and experience.
das **Zeugnis**, Zeugnisse	certificate, diploma
das **Schulzeugnis**, -zeugnisse	school diploma, school-leaving certificate
das **Arbeitsleben**	working life

A9

stolz	proud

4 Hochschulstudium – und dann?

das **Hochschulstudium**	college or university studies

A10

der **Lebenslauf**, -läufe	curriculum vitae
der **Ausbildungsweg**, -wege	education and training
die **Anschrift**, Anschriften	address
das **Geburtsdatum**	date of birth
der **Geburtsort**	place of birth
schulisch	school
die **Grundschule**, -schulen	elementary school
der **Abschluss**, Abschlüsse	completion of school, graduation
das **Abitur**	college-preparatory high-school diploma
die **Baumschule**, -schulen	nursery
der **Gehilfe**, Gehilfen	assistant
die **Baumschulgehilfen-prüfung**	nursery assistant's examination
die **Fachhochschule**, -hochschulen	college for specialized training, polytechnic
die **Fachrichtung**, -richtungen	academic field, subject
der **Gartenbau**	horticulture
die **Universität**, Universitäten	university
abschließen	to complete, to finish
einschreiben, sich	to register, to enroll

A12

die **Berufschance**, -chancen	career chance
einschätzen	to estimate, to assess
der **Absolvent**, Absolventen	graduate
der **Hochschulabsolvent**, -absolventen	college or university graduate
die **Studiensituation**	situation for college or university students

die **Arbeitssituation**	labor situation, job situation
der **Akademiker**, Akademiker	academic
die **Hochschule**, Hochschulen	institution of higher education
der **Berufsanfänger**, -anfänger	beginner in a career or profession
der **Hochschulabschluss**, -abschlüsse	college or university degree
die **Dauerstelle**, -stellen	permanent position
zunächst	at first
der **Vertrag**, Verträge	contract
das **Unternehmen**, Unternehmen	company, firm
schulen	to train
der **Uni-Absolvent**, -Absolventen	university graduate
das **Praktikum**, Praktika	traineeship
der **Kursleiter**, -leiter	course leader
einstellen	to hire
Berufsanfänger einstellen	to hire beginners
bewähren, sich	to prove oneself

5 Das Bewerbungsgespräch

das **Bewerbungs-gespräch**, -gespräche	job interview

A13

die **Gesprächssituation**, -situationen	conversation situation
die **Haltung**	stance
die **Körperhaltung**	posture
die **Mimik**	gestures and facial expressions

A14

bisherig	previous
die **Tätigkeit**, Tätigkeiten	activity, employment, work
zukünftig	future
bewerben, sich	to apply
die **Bürokauffrau**, -frauen	licensed office secretary or bookkeeper
das **Telefonat**, Telefonate	telephone conversation
die **Krankenkasse**, -kassen	medical insurance
die **Anfrage**, Anfragen	enquiry
der/die **Kranke**, die Kranken	sick person
der **Service**	service
der **Kunden-Service**	customer service
die **Reklamation**, Reklamationen	complaint
der **PC**, Pcs (= Personal-Computer)	PC

die **Bewerbung**, Bewerbungen	application
telefonisch	(by) telephone
absagen	to cancel
das **Arbeitszeugnis**, -zeugnisse	reference from an employer
tätig	active
die **Bezahlung**	pay

A15

aussehen	to look
Wie sieht es mit der Bezahlung aus?	What about the pay?
die **Arbeitszeit**, -zeiten	working hours
die **Anforderung**, Anforderungen	demand, requirement, qualification
die **Kenntnisse** (Pl.)	knowledge
die **Geschäftszeit**, -zeiten	business hours
die **Bürozeit**, -zeiten	office hours
das **Gehalt**, Gehälter	salary

6 Aussprache

A16

stimmhaft	voiced
stimmlos	voiceless
das **Silbenende**	end of the syllable

A18

die **Häufung**	heap, cluster
die **Konsonanten-häufung**	consonant cluster
das **Schulsystem**, -systeme	school system
die **Hauptschule**, -schulen	basic secondary and vocational school
die **Arbeitsvermittlung**	job referral
die **Gehaltsvorstellung**, -vorstellungen	salary expectation
der **Zwischenvokal**, -vokale	intermediary vowel

7 Wortschatz

A19

das **Wortfeld**, Wortfelder	word field
die **Lehre**, Lehren	apprenticeship
kreativ	creative
in die Lehre gehen	to become an apprentice
der **Schwerpunkt**, -punkte	main focus, area of concentration
selbst Schwerpunkte setzen	to set up one's own areas of concentration

A20		
das **Schema**, Schemata	pattern, diagram	

8 Grammatik

das **Partizip I**	present participle
frustrieren	to frustrate
frustrierend	frustrating
frustrierende Jobs für Absolventen	frustrating jobs for graduates
nominal	nominal
nominale Gruppen im Satz	nominal groups in the sentence

das **Attribut**, Attribute	attribute
das **Linksattribut**, -attribute	pre-nominal attribute
das **Rechtsattribut**, -attribute	post-nominal attribute
der **Arbeitsmarkt**	job market
das **Genitiv-Attribut**, -Attribute	genitive attribute
das **Präpositional-Attribut**, -Attribute	prepositional attribute
die **Strafe**, Strafen	punishment
das **Wunder**, Wunder	wonder
kein Wunder, dass...	no wonder...

27 Beruf: Malerin

1 „Jede Form ist vielseitig"

vielseitig	many-sided
Jede Form ist vielseitig.	Every form is many-sided.

A1

die **Abbildung**, Abbildungen	reproduction
das **Gemälde**, Gemälde	painting
beunruhigend	disturbing
dramatisch	dramatic

A2

die **Malerei**, Malereien	painting
das **Lieblingsbild**	favorite picture
klassisch	classical
die **Plastik**, Plastiken	sculpture
das **Porträt**, Porträts	portrait

A3

das **Zitat**, Zitate	quotation
ästhetisch	aesthetic
der **Wert**, Werte	value
einen bestimmten ästhetischen Wert haben	to have a certain aesthetic value
die **Begabung**, Begabungen	talent, gift
besondere	special
eine besondere Begabung	a special gift
die **Literatur**, Literaturen	literature
fördern	to foster, to support
bilden	to form
die bildende Kunst	plastic art, fine art
der **Kunstgegenstand**, -gegenstände	art object
das **Handwerk**	craft
das **Kunsthandwerk**	arts and crafts
das **Kunstlied**, -lieder	art song
allerlei	all kinds of

das **Gemäuer**, Gemäuer	walls
allerlei Gemäuer	all kinds of walls
hineinschauen	to look into, to look at
vielfach	multiple, many kinds of
der **Fleck**, Flecken	stain
beschmutzen	to make dirty
die **Ähnlichkeit**, Ähnlichkeiten	similarity
der **Fels**, Felsen	rock, cliff

2 „Malen ist wie Auf-die-Welt-bringen"

auf die Welt bringen	to give birth

A4

der **Arbeitsplatz**, -plätze	workplace
das **Atelier**, Ateliers	studio
die **Ostschweiz**	eastern Switzerland
die **Matura** (österr., schweiz. = Abitur)	(Austrian-Swiss) college-preparatory high-school diploma
die **Suche**	search
auf der Suche sein	to seek
der **Ausgleich**	emotional outlet, compensation
der **Zeichenkurs**, -kurse	drawing class
zum Ausgleich Zeichenkurse geben	to compensate by giving drawing courses
organisch	organic
weich	soft, gentle

A5

der **Prozess**, Prozesse	process
der **Arbeitsprozess**, -prozesse	work process
strukturieren	to structure
die **Maltechnik**, -techniken	painting technique

3 Vorbereitung einer Ausstellung

die **Vorbereitung**, Vorbereitungen	preparation
die **Ausstellung**, Ausstellungen	exhibition

A7

die **Künstlerin**, Künstlerinnen	artist
verpacken	to pack
streichen	to paint
die **Presse**	press (newspapers etc.)
schicken	to send
der **Druck**	print
Versand	shipment
die **Architektur**	architecture
das **Verhältnis**	relationship
Architektur im Verhältnis zur Natur	architecture in relationship to nature
die **Phase**, Phasen	phase
Bilder der neuesten Phase	pictures from the latest phase
die **Produzentengalerie**	Producers' Gallery
die **Kapsel**, Kapseln	capsule
die **Schale**, Schalen	shell
gegenständlich	representational
Sie ist keine gegenständliche Malerin.	She is not a representational painter.
die **Reduktion**, Reduktionen	reduction
entgegensetzen	to contrast (with)

A8

die **Verabredung**, Verabredungen	arrangement, date
die **Eröffnung**, Eröffnungen	opening
stattfinden	to take place
ausstellen	to exhibit

4 Die Eröffnung

A9

sortieren	to sort (out), to arrange
die **Überzeugung**	conviction
das **Genie**, Genies	genius
das **Motiv**, Motive	motif
der **Impressionismus**	Impressionism
der **Expressionismus**	Expressionism
scheußlich	terrible, awful
das **Gegenteil**	opposite, contrary
Ganz im Gegenteil!	On the contrary!

5 Aussprache

A11

zusammenfassen	to put together

die **Sinngruppe**, -gruppen	sense group, related-word group

A12

der **Rückfragesatz**, -sätze	sentence with request for repetition or clarification

6 Wortschatz

A14

das **Standbild**, Standbilder	statue
die **Regie**	direction
Regie führen	to direct
der **Regisseur**, Regisseure	director
die **Regisseurin**, Regisseurinnen	director
der **Führer**, Führer (= Museumsführer)	docent
treten	to step
das **Denkmal**, Denkmäler	monument
errichten	to erect
verhindern	to prevent

A15

das **Wortschatzspiel**, -spiele	vocabulary game
würfeln	to throw dice
ziehen	to proceed, to go
die **Reihe**	row
der Reihe nach	one after the other
einsperren	to lock in
die **Runde**, Runden	turn
aussetzen	to miss
Eine Runde aussetzen!	Miss a turn!
schenken	to give as a present
das **Feld**, Felder	space
Drei Felder vor!	Advance three spaces!
fotografieren	to photograph
der **Brunnen**, Brunnen	fountain

7 Grammatik

die **Direktivergänzung**, -ergänzungen	adjunct of direction
fakultativ	optional
eine fakultative Ergänzung	an optional completion
die **Angabe**, Angaben	information, indication
der **Satzkern**	sentence core
der **Satzbau**	sentence structure
das **Vorfeld**	initial position in the sentence
das **Mittelfeld**	middle position in the sentence
finit	finite
die finite Form des Verbs	finite form of the verb
die **Wortbildung**	word formation

1 Beruf: Berufung oder Job?

die **Berufung**	calling

A1

durchschnittlich	average
der **Verdienst**	earnings
durchschnittlicher Verdienst pro Monat	average earnings per month
der **Arzt**, Ärzte	doctor, physician
die **Ärztin**, Ärztinnen	doctor, physician
die **Krankenschwester**, -schwestern	nurse
der **Krankenpfleger**, -pfleger	male nurse
die **Bäuerin**, Bäuerinnen	farmer
die **Bäckerin**, Bäckerinnen	baker
der **Polizist**, Polizisten	policeman
die **Polizistin**, Polizistinnen	policewoman
die **Politikerin**, Politikerinnen	politician
der **Profisportler**, -sportler	professional athlete
die **Profisportlerin**, -sportlerinnen	professional athlete

A2

der **Berufswunsch**, -wünsche	career wish
das **Wort**, Worte	word
ohne Worte	without words
frei	free
in der freien Natur	in the open countryside
das **Team**, Teams	team
im Team arbeiten	to work in a team
der **Traktor**, Traktoren	tractor
das **Instrument**, Instrumente	instrument

A3

erlernen	to learn (completely or thoroughly)
notwendig	necessary
das **Übel**, Übel	evil
ein notwendiges Übel zum Geldverdienen	a necessary evil in order to earn money
der **Verstand**	understanding
ein gesunder Menschenverstand	common sense
vertrauen	to trust
die **Intuition**	intuition
anpassungsfähig	able to adapt
diplomatisch	diplomatic
die **Disziplin**	discipline
die **Selbstdisziplin**	self-discipline

hilfsbereit	helpful
leisten, sich	to afford
sich etwas leisten können	to afford things

2 Stellenangebote und Stellengesuche

das **Stellenangebot**, -angebote	job offer
das **Stellengesuch**, -gesuche	job search

A4

die **Anzeige**, Anzeigen	advertisement
die **Stellenanzeige**, -anzeigen	job advertisement
auswerten	to analyze, to evaluate

1

die **PC-Kenntnisse** (Pl.)	computer skills
die **Fremdsprachenkenntnisse** (Pl.)	foreign language proficiency
die **Büroerfahrung**, -erfahrungen	office experience
verfügen	to have (at one's disposal)
über Büroerfahrung verfügen	to have office experience
bieten	to offer
abwechslungsreich	varied, diverse
der **Bürojob**, -jobs	office job
die **Semesterferien** (Pl.)	vacation (school, university etc.)

2

die **Fachabteilung**, -abteilungen	department
leiten	to lead
die leitende Ärztin	senior physician, head physician
die **Hals-Nasen-Ohrenkrankheiten** (Pl.)	ear, nose, and throat illnesses
derzeit	at the present time
umfangreich	extensive
die **Ambulanz**, Ambulanzen	outpatient clinic

3

der **Bürokaufmann**, -kaufmänner	licensed office secretary or bookkeeper
die **Bürokraft**, Bürokräfte	office worker
das **Lagerhaus**, Lagerhäuser	warehouse
das **Sägewerk**, -werke	sawmill

4

der **Sitz**, Sitze	headquarters
eine Firma mit Sitz in . . .	a firm with its headquarters in . . .

die **Telefonistin**, Telefonistinnen	switchboard operator, telephone receptionist
der **Telefonist**, Telefonisten	switchboard operator, telephone receptionist
die **Stellung**	position
die **Halbtagsstellung**	half-day position
der **Dienst**, Dienste	service, work
der **Wechseldienst**	shift-work
die **Grundkenntnisse** (Pl.)	basic knowledge
voraussetzen	to require
von Vorteil sein	to be of advantage
das **Lichtbild**, -bilder	photograph

5

medizinisch-chirurgisch	medical and surgical
der **Bereich**, Bereiche	sphere, field
im medizinisch-chirurgischen Bereich	in the medical and surgical field
eintreten	to enter
in ein bestehendes Team eintreten	to enter an already existing team
die **Unterlagen** (Pl.)	documents, papers
die **Bewerbungs-unterlagen** (Pl.)	application and supporting material
die **Unternehmens-beratung**	management consultant

6

die **Teilzeit**	part-time
langjährig	of many years
die **Berufserfahrung**	work experience
belastbar	able to work under pressure
eine neue Aufgabe suchen	to seek a new position

7

das **Allround-Talent**, -Talente	all-round talent
sportlich	athletic
witzig	witty, with a sense of humor
die **Branche**, Branchen	branch, industry
die **Filmbranche**	film industry
die **Werbebranche**	advertising industry
die **Touristikbranche**	tourist industry

8

der **Landwirt**, Landwirte	farmer
die **Landwirtin**, Landwirtinnen	farmer

9

separat	separate
separates Einzelzimmer	separate room of one's own

10

der **Diplom-Übersetzer**, -Übersetzer	university graduate in translation
die **Diplom-Übersetzerin**, -Übersetzerinnen	university graduate in translation

ungekündigt	not having been given notice
in ungekündigter Stellung	with a postion which has not been terminated
die **Fluggesellschaft**, -gesellschaften	airline
zuverlässig	reliable
verantwortungsvoll	trustworthy, responsible

11

kinderlieb	fond of children
die **Haushaltshilfe**	home help, housemaid
der **Zuschuss**, Zuschüsse	subsidy, allowance
der **Fahrtkostenzuschuss**	travel allowance, travel expenses

A5

der **Bewerber**, Bewerber	applicant
die **Bewerberin**, Bewerberinnen	applicant

3 Berufsalltag

A7

der **Arbeitsplatz**, -plätze	workplace
der **Lohn**, Löhne	wage
die **Schiene**, Schienen	rail
der **InterCity-Express**	InterCity express train
die **Zugbegleiterin**, -begleiterinnen	(train) conductor
balancieren	to balance
das **Tablett**, Tabletts	tray
der **Gang**, Gänge	aisle
Sie balanciert ein Tablett mit Kaffee über den Gang.	She balances a tray with coffee in the aisle.
servieren	to serve
brutto	gross
der **Zuschlag**, Zuschläge	extra pay
der **Wochenend-zuschlag**, -zuschläge	extra pay for weekend duty
der **Nachtzuschlag**, -zuschläge	extra pay for night duty
der **Zugbegleiter**, Zugbegleiter	(train) conductor
der **Lebensrhythmus**	rhythm of life
-tägig	-day
elftägig	eleven-day
der **Dienstplan**, -pläne	work schedule, work cycle
bestimmen	to determine
Der Lebensrhythmus wird vom elftägigen Dienstplan bestimmt.	Her rhythm of life is determined by the eleven-day work cycle.
der **Heimatbahnhof**	home train-station
übernachten	to spend the night
verabreden, sich	to arrange to meet

andererseits — on the other hand
einteilen (sich) — to divide up, to arrange
Ich kann mir die Tage so einteilen, wie ich möchte. — I can arrange the days as I like.

A8
die **Pilotin**, Pilotinnen — pilot
der **Steward**, Stewards — steward
die **Stewardess**, Stewardessen — stewardess
anstrengend — strenuous, taxing

A9
der **Berufsalltag** — daily work routine

4 Die Arbeitswelt von morgen

die **Arbeitswelt** — working world
Arbeitswelt im Wandel — working world in transition

A10
die **Prognose**, Prognosen — prognosis
der **Arbeitnehmer**, -nehmer — employee
das **Berufsleben** — professional life, working life
arbeitslos — unemployed
der/die **Angestellte**, die Angestellten — employee
entlassen — to discharge, to fire
der **Abstand**, Abstände — gap
der/die **Arbeitslose**, die Arbeitslosen — unemployed person
privat — private
die **Service-Firma**, -Firmen — private service firms
eine große Rolle spielen — to play a large role

A11
das **Konzept**, Konzepte — concept
das **Geschäftskonzept**, -konzepte — business concept
die **Zielgruppe**, -gruppen — target group
das **Werbemittel**, -mittel — means of advertising
die **„Rot Runners"** (Pl.) — pun combining "rot" (red) and "road runner"
der **Kurierdienst**, -dienste — messenger service
umweltfreundlich — environment-friendly
flitzen — to dash
der **Kurier**, Kuriere — courier, messenger
das **Rennrad**, -räder — racing bike
das **Funkgerät**, Funkgeräte — radio
die **Taxizentrale**, -zentralen — taxi company central office
der **Mitgründer**, Mitgründer — co-founder
sich etwas träumen lassen — to dream of something

A12
die **„Trouble Shooters"** (Pl.) — "Trouble Shooters"
die **Geburtstagsfeier**, -feiern — birthday party
die **Maschine**, Maschinen — machine
die **Waschmaschine**, -maschinen — washing machine
der **Geschäftstermin**, -termine — business appointment
die **Privatperson**, -personen — private person
absolut — absolute
erledigen — to take care of
die **Farbkopie**, -kopien — color copy
die **Filmproduktion**, -produktionen — film production

5 Aussprache

A13
emotional — emotional
ärgerlich — annoying, irritating
Das ist aber ärgerlich! — Now that's really annoying!

A14
zusammensetzen — to put together
zusammengesetzte Verben — compound verbs

6 Wortschatz

A15
das **Management** — management
der/die **Vorgesetzte**, die Vorgesetzten — superior
die **Beamtin**, Beamtinnen — official
einsatzfreudig — enthusiastic, eager to contribute
teamorientiert — team-oriented
lernfähig — able to learn
das **Organisationstalent**, -talente — talent for organization
die **Internet-Kenntnisse** (Pl.) — Internet skills
der **Führerschein**, Führerscheine — driver's license
die **Herausforderung**, Herausforderungen — challenge
die **Sprachkenntnisse** (Pl.) — foreign language skills
entscheiden — to decide, to make decisions
verteilen — to distribute
beschäftigen, sich — to occupy oneself with, to deal with

das **Vertrauen**	trust
fordern	to demand
die **Dienstleistung**, Dienstleistungen	service
umsetzen	to realize, to put into action

A16

der **Lückentext**, -texte	cloze text
die **Jobsuche**	job search
die **Unterhaltung**, Unterhaltungen	conversation
die **Erzählung**, Erzählungen	story

die **Reaktion**, Reaktionen	reaction
die **Bitte**, Bitten	request

7 Grammatik

das **Lebewesen**, Lebewesen	living being
das **Pronominaladverb**, -adverbien	pronominal adverb
das **Signal**, Signale	signal
das **Futur I**	future tense
beschleunigen	to speed up, to accelerate

29 Wien

1 „Wien, Wien, nur du allein..."

A2

die **Tourismus-Werbung**, -Werbungen	tourism advertisement
charmant	charming
die charmanteste Hauptstadt der Welt	the most charming capital city in the world
der **Winkel**, Winkel	nook, corner
die **Prunkstraße**, -straßen	magnificent boulevard
die **Hofburg**	Hofburg Palace (of the Austrian Emperors)
der **Heldenplatz**	Heroes' Square
der **Dom**, Dome	Cathedral
das **Beisel**, Beisel (wienerisch = Gasthaus)	(Austrian) simple restaurant with local clientele
das **Kaffeehaus**, -häuser	coffee house
sprichwörtlich	proverbial
wienerisch	Viennese
die **Geselligkeit**	conviviality
die **Gemütlichkeit**	coziness, warmth
anziehend	attractive
Die sprichwörtliche Wiener Geselligkeit und Gemütlichkeit macht diese Stadt so anziehend.	The proverbial Viennese conviviality and warmth makes this city so attractive.
die **Kaiserin**, Kaiserinnen	empress
das Kaiserin-"Sissi"-Denkmal	the monument to Empress "Sissi"
die **Secession**	"the Secession" (avantgarde artists of the 1890s)
der **Jugendstil**	Art Nouveau
der **Volksgarten**	the Volksgarten (public park in Vienna)
der **Prater**	the Prater (public park in Vienna)
das **Riesenrad**	Ferris wheel

A3

die **Ansage**, Ansagen	announcement
die **Station**, Stationen	station, stop

A4

beziehen, sich	to refer
der **Prospekttext**, -texte	text in the brochure
Sie bezieht sich auf den Prospekttext.	She refers to the text in the brochure.
das **Stadtprogramm**, -programme	schedule of events in the city
die **Wärme**	warmth
die **Herzlichkeit**	cordiality, heartiness
die **Gleichgültigkeit**	indifference
das **Tempo**	tempo, pace
die **Hektik**	hectic rush, frantic pace
das **Alltagsbild**	everyday life, everyday scene
die **Kulisse**, Kulissen	backdrop, scenery
missen	to miss, to go without
Ich möchte die Sehenswürdigkeiten nicht missen.	I wouldn't like to go without these sights.
genauso wenig	just as little, just as unwillingly
die **Aktivität**, Aktivitäten	activity
kulturelle Aktivitäten in Wien	cultural life in Vienna
lebendig	alive, pulsating, vibrant
der **Schmäh** (österr.)	(Viennese) snide humor
der sprichwörtliche Wiener Schmäh	the proverbial Viennese "Schmäh"
erwähnen	to mention
die **Einstellung**, Einstellungen	view, attitude
die **Lebenseinstellung**	view of life, philosophy of life
Schmäh führen (österr.)	(Austrian) to talk "Schmäh," to make snide jokes

blödeln	to fool around, to make silly jokes
der **Heurige**, die Heurigen (österr.)	(Austrian) new wine from the current year, or an inn which serves such wine
apropos	apropos, speaking of

A5

das **Hörbild**, Hörbilder	picture in sounds

2 Das Kaffeehaus – zwischen Mythos und Wirklichkeit

A6

ablenken, sich	to divert oneself, to amuse oneself
beruhigen, sich	to calm down
das **Denkhandwerk**	the craft of thinking
die **Gesellschaft**	company
Im Kaffeehaus sitzen Leute, die Gesellschaft brauchen.	People who need company sit in the coffee house.
die **Aufsuchung**, Aufsuchungen	visit
sachlich	objective, practical, serious
kennzeichnen	to mark, to characterize
von einem Wunsch gekennzeichnet sein	to be characterized by a wish
ferner	moreover, in addition
beklagen, sich	to complain

A7

das **Publikum**	patrons, customers
die **Öffnungszeit**, -zeiten	opening times, business hours
unaufdringlich	unobtrusive
der **Nerv**, Nerven	nerve
niemand auf die Nerven gehen	to not get on anybody's nerves
vollkommen	complete
ungestört	undisturbed
plaudern	to chat
die **Institution**, Institutionen	institution
der **Bezirk**, Bezirke	district
der **Schachspieler**, -spieler	chess player
der **Kartenspieler**, -spieler	card player
das **Extrazimmer**, -zimmer	extra room
der/die **Berufstätige**, die Berufstätigen	working person
der **Pensionist**, Pensionisten	retired person
das **Tagespublikum**	day customers
das **Nachtpublikum**	night customers
unterscheiden, sich	to be different
vornehm	genteel, upper-class
die vornehme Gesellschaft	upper-class society

österreichisch	Austrian
österreichische Tageszeitungen	Austrian daily newspapers
die **FAZ** (= Frankfurter Allgemeine Zeitung)	German daily newspaper *Frankfurter Allgemeine Zeitung*
die **Süddeutsche** (= die Süddeutsche Zeitung)	German daily newspaper *Süddeutsche Zeitung*
die **Neue Zürcher** (Neue Zürcher Zeitung)	Swiss daily newspaper *Neue Zürcher Zeitung*
der **Mocca**, Moccas	mocha
die **Melange** (österr.)	coffee with plenty of milk
verlangen	to ask for, to order (food etc.)
der **Einspänner** (österr.)	black coffee with whipped cream

A8

das **Stammcafé**, -cafés	cafe where one is a regular customer

3 Ein Platz und seine Geschichte

A10

der **Held**, Helden	hero
grandios	magnificent
das **Monument**, Monumente	monument
das **Reitermonument**, -monumente	equestrian monument
majestätisch	majestic
die **Residenz**, Residenzen	palace
der **Kaiser**, die Kaiser	emperor
der **Glanz**	brilliance, splendor
die **Größe**	greatness
die **Monarchie**, Monarchien	monarchy
Glanz und Größe der österreichischen Monarchie	splendor and greatness of the Austrian monarchy
befinden, sich	to be situated, to be housed
der **Amtssitz**	official residence
der **Bundespräsident**, -präsidenten	federal president
„**der Führer**" (von Adolf Hitler selbst geschaffene Bezeichnung)	the "Leader" (Hitler's self-designated title)
der **Kanzler**, Kanzler	chancellor
nationalsozialistisch	National Socialist
das **Reich**, Reiche	empire
das **Nationalsozialistische Deutsche Reich**	National Socialist German Reich
verkünden	to proclaim
der **Anschluss**	forced political union of Austria with Germany in 1938
der **Eintritt**	entry

unbeschreiblich	indescribable
der **Jubel**	jubilation
die **Botschaft**, Botschaften	message
die **Kundgebung**, Kundgebungen	statement, demonstration
der **Ausländerhass**	hatred of foreigners
der **Rechtsradikalismus**	rightist extremism
die Kundgebung gegen Ausländerhass und Rechtsradikalismus	demonstration against rightist extremism and hatred of foreigners
beeindruckend	impressive
der **Organisator**, Organisatoren	organizer
der **Mitorganisator**, -organisatoren	co-organizer
der **Schrecken**	terror, horror
die **Rede**, Reden	speech
der **Friedensnobelpreisträger**, -träger	Nobel Peace Prize winner
die **Vernichtung**	annihilation
die **Begeisterung**	enthusiasm
der **Zuhörer**, Zuhörer	listener
ermöglichen	to make possible
die **Solidarität**	solidarity
der/die **Bedrohte**, die Bedrohten	threatened person
das **Dritte Reich** (1933–1945)	the Third Reich

4 Aussprache

A12

der **Anlaut**	initial sound
das **Klischee**, Klischees	cliché
der **Knall**	crash, bang
die **Schreibweise**	spelling

A13

der **Inlaut**	medial sound
der **Apfelstrudel**, -strudel	apple strudel
kunsthistorisch	art historical

der **Topfenstrudel**, -strudel	strudel with sweetened cottage cheese filling

A14

der **Auslaut**	terminal sound
brummen	to mumble, to mutter
knurren	to growl
murren	to grumble

5 Wortschatz

A15

das **Gegensatzpaar**, -paare	pair of opposites
das **Antonym**, Antonyme	antonym
das **Synonym**, Synonyme	synonym
gegensätzlich	opposite
geduldig	patient
kompliziert	complicated

A17

das **Spital**, Spitäler (österr., schweiz.)	(Swiss-Austrian) hospital
das **Parlament**, Parlamente	parliament
die **Nationalbibliothek**	national library
die **Schnellbahn**, Schnellbahnen	commuter train
die **Netzkarte**, Netzkarten	unlimited ticket (for public transportation)
die **Hausmannskost**	simple home cooking

A18

der **Großstadtverkehr**	city traffic

6 Grammatik

der **Konjunktiv I**	present subjunctive
die **Redewiedergabe**	reported speech
die **Perspektive**, Perspektiven	perspective
der **Ersatz**	replacement
verpassen	to miss

30 Die Perlenkette

S. 114

die **Kette**, Ketten	chain, necklace
die **Perlenkette**, -ketten	pearl necklace

A1

die **Kriminalfall**, -fälle	criminal case
jeweils	each time
blättern	to turn pages
zurückblättern	to leaf back
der **Detektiv**, Detektive	detective

der **Privatdetektiv**, -detektive	private detective
der **Fall**, Fälle	case
das **Köpfchen**	a little intelligence, brains
viel Köpfchen brauchen	to need some brains
nebenbei	also, while doing so

A2

überqueren	to cross
der **Bass**, Bässe	bass

wummern	to thrum
das **Echo**, Echos	echo
zurückwerfen	to throw back
Das Echo wirft die Musik zurück.	The music rebounds with the echo.
die **Fahrradtour**, -touren	bicycle tour
verschreiben	to prescribe
ratlos	at a loss
verständlich	comprehensible
sich verständlich machen	to make oneself understood
die **Parade**, Paraden	parade
die **Liebes-Parade**	Love Parade
papageienbunt	as colorful as a parrot
fassen	to grasp, to take hold of
jemand an den Armen fassen	to take hold of someone by the arms
mitziehen	to pull along with
schaden	to harm, to hurt
festhalten	to hold tight
sich an etwas festhalten	to hold on tight to something
das **Fahrradfahren**	bicycling

S. 115

A4

die **Sekretärin**, Sekretärinnen	secretary
das **Piepsen**	to squeak, to peep, to beep
einstecken	to take something along, to put in one's pocket
die **Sauna**, Saunas	sauna
die **Ecke**, Ecken	corner, nook
eine ruhige Ecke suchen	to look for a quiet nook
dranbleiben (am Telefon)	to stay on the (telephone) line
der **Gehsteig**, Gehsteige	sidewalk
die **Seitenstraße**, -straßen	side street
die **Einfahrt**, Einfahrten	driveway
entschließen, sich	to decide
kurz entschlossen	on the spur of the moment
abstellen	to put down, to park
Er stellt sein Rad ab.	He parks his bike.
betreten	to enter
einen Laden betreten	to enter a store

A5

die **Tanzbewegung**, -bewegungen	dance movement
das **Gleichgewicht**	equilibrium

A6

radeln	to cycle, to ride one's bike
der **Schulfreund**, -freunde	friend from school
der **Klassenprimus**	best in the class

der **Streber**, Streber	annoyingly ambitious person
verlieren	to lose
sich aus den Augen verlieren	to lose sight of someone
das **Abiturfest**, -feste	class reunion ("Gymnasium")
die **Glatze**, Glatzen	bald head
schlau	clever, sly
der **Geschäftsmann**, -männer	businessman
das **Gitter**, Gitter	grid
das **Plastikgitter**, -gitter	plastic grid
montieren	to mount, to install
einbrechen	to break in, to commit burglary
rein	pure, mere
die **Vorsichtsmaßnahme**, -maßnahmen	precautionary measure
eine reine Vorsichtsmaßnahme	merely a precautionary measure
vorbeikommen	to pass by, to come by
kichern	to giggle
ein Mädchen für alles	girl Friday
bestens	very well
der **olle Bergmann** (berlinerisch)	(Berlin dialect) Old Man Bergmann
zucken	to shrug
die **Schulter**, Schultern	shoulder
die Schultern zucken	to shrug one's shoulders

A7

das **Schmuckgeschäft**, -geschäfte	jewelry store
hinausgehen	to go out
schütteln	to shake
den Kopf schütteln	to shake one's head
greifen	to take hold of, to grab
zum Telefon greifen	to grab the telephone

S. 116

A8

warme Küche	hot meals
hervorragend	excellent, outstanding
der/die **Büroangestellte**, die -angestellten	office worker
der **Rechtsanwalt**, Rechtsanwälte	attorney
der **Architekt**, Architekten	architect
die **Bar**, Bars	bar
verraten	to reveal
der **Geheimtipp**, -tipps	secret tip
Wir verraten einen Geheimtipp.	We reveal a secret tip.

die **Biergarten-Gemütlichkeit**	the relaxed and friendly atmosphere of a beer garden
der **Bistro-Stil**	bistro style
widersprechen	to contradict
wegbewegen, sich	to move away from
der **Schritt**, Schritte	step, pace
der **Ku'damm** (= Kurfürstendamm)	Kurfürstendamm (famous street in Berlin)
der **Kiez** (berlinerisch)	(Berlin dialect) neighborhood (where one feels at home)
das **Kiezgefühl**	(Berlin dialect) homey neighborhood atmosphere

A9

verrückt	crazy
die **Hitze**	heat
zupfen	to tug, to pull
kleiden, sich	to dress oneself
vorübergehen	to pass
das **Pils**, Pils	Pilsner beer
langweilen, sich	to be bored
herumstehen	to stand around
das **Foyer**, Foyers	foyer
eilen	to hurry
ausstrecken	to stretch out
der **Smoking**, Smokings	dinner jacket, tuxedo
peinlich	embarrassing, awkward
der **Geschäftspartner**, -partner	business partner
deuten	to point
Müller deutet auf sein leeres Glas.	Müller points to his empty glass.
der **Kellner**, Kellner	waiter
nicken	to nod

S. 117

A10

der **Safe**, Safes	safe
sichern	to secure
die **Anleitung**, Anleitungen	instruction
wertvoll	valuable
verschwinden	to disappear
die **Codenummer**, -nummern	code number
sich etwas merken	to note, to remember
das **Notizbuch**, -bücher	notebook
das **Prinzip**, Prinzipien	principle
im Prinzip schon	in principle yes
das **Liebhaberstück**, -stücke	collector's item
die **Perle**, Perlen	pearl

reinweiß	pure white
die **Goldfassung**, -fassungen	gold setting
der **Liebhaber**, Liebhaber	connoisseur, collector
versichern	to insure
Ist die Kette versichert?	Is the necklace insured?
die **Diskretion**	discretion
Äußerste Diskretion!	Absolute discretion!
wischen	to wipe
der **Schweiß**	sweat
die **Stirn**, Stirnen	forehead
der **Hinterkopf**, -köpfe	back of one's head
reichen	to reach
Er wischt sich den Schweiß aus der Stirn, die fast bis zum Hinterkopf reicht.	He wipes the sweat from his forehead, which reaches almost to the back of his head.
austrinken	to drink up, to finish drinking

A11

die **Zigarette**, Zigaretten	cigarette
die **Packung**, Packungen	pack
das **Feuer**	light
die **Terrasse**, Terrassen	terrace
die **Platzangst**	claustrophobia
kritisch	critical
Er schaut ihn kritisch an.	He gives him a critical look.
die Techno-Sch . . . (Scheiße)	techno-sh - t
reingeraten	mixed up in something, caught up in something
Ich bin da zufällig reingeraten.	I got caught up in it by accident.
erstaunlich	astonishing
der **Pazifist**, Pazifisten	pacifist
der **Hippie**, Hippies	hippie
der **Alt-Hippie**, -Hippies	former hippie, aging hippie
die **Tonne**, Tonnen (= t)	(metric) ton
entsorgen	to dispose of
der **Traumtänzer**, -tänzer	dreamer, fantasizer
der **Dreck**	filth, waste
sich einen Dreck um etwas kümmern	to not give a damn about something

S. 118

die **Kunstaktion**, -aktionen	art campaign, innovative art program
innovativ	innovative
o Gott!	Oh, God!
die **Kunstgeschichte**	art history
brotlos	unremunerative

eine brotlose Kunst	a job or profession with no money in it
einsteigen	to get in, to climb in
Er wollte, dass ich in seinen Laden einsteige.	He wanted me to go to work in his store.
die **Betriebswirtschaft**	business administration
klopfen	to knock, to slap
auf die Schulter klopfen	to slap someone on the shoulder

A13

das **Befinden**	state of health
gnädig	gracious, kind
die gnädige Frau	dear lady, madam
zögern	to hesitate
der **Schwiegersohn**, -söhne	son-in-law
autsch!	Ouch!
Verzeihung!	Pardon me!
kräftig	strong, powerful
der **Händedruck**	handshake
das **Training**	training
voll im Training sein	to be in top condition
Karate	karate
fit halten	to keep fit
sauber	clean, nice (negative or sarcastic)
mein sauberer Herr Schwiegersohn	my "dear" son-in-law
der **Geschäftsfreund**, -freunde	business associate, business crony
aufregend	exciting, agitating
abschieben	to deport, to shove or get out of the way
verstorben	deceased, late
der **Taugenichts**, Taugenichtse	good-for-nothing
lächerlich	ridiculous
die **Osterinsel**	Easter Island
das **Eisen**	iron
zum alten Eisen gehören	to be ready for the scrap heap
schütteln	to shake
die Hand schütteln	to shake the hand
davonspazieren	to walk away

A14

entdecken	to discover

S. 119

attraktiv	attractive
mittler-	middle-
eine Dame mittleren Alters	a middle-aged lady
das **Weinglas**, -gläser	wine glass
anstoßen	to clink glasses

halt	you know, simply, just
erholen, sich	to recover, to rest
braun gebrannt	suntanned
der **Charmeur**, Charmeure	charmer
das **Häuschen**, Häuschen	little house, cottage
Sehr erfreut!	Pleased to meet you!
Encantado! (span.)	Pleased to meet you!
um Gottes willen!	For Heaven's sake!
der **Langweiler**, Langweiler	bore
vermissen	to miss
das **Gedächtnis**	memory

A16

die **Gewohnheit**, Gewohnheiten	habit
die **Lesegewohnheit**, -gewohnheiten	reading habit
die **Bemerkung**, Bemerkungen	remark
der **Ehemann**, -männer	husband
reizend	charming
stören	to disturb
der **Ausgang**, Ausgänge	exit

A17

ordnen	to arrange, to order
der **Charakter**	character, nature
Die Polizei lobt den friedlichen Charakter der Veranstaltung.	The police praise the peaceful nature of the event.
die **Sportseite**, -seiten (Übers.: in der Zeitung)	sports page
der **Polizeibericht**, -berichte	police report
der **Unglücksfall**, -fälle	accident
das **Verbrechen**, Verbrechen	crime
der **Einbruch**, Einbrüche	break-in, burglary
der **Diebstahl**, Diebstähle	theft
weglegen	to put away
schließlich	after all
der **Notizblock**, -blöcke	notebook
der **Jogging-Anzug**, -Anzüge	jogging suit
die **Versicherung**, Versicherungen	insurance
das **Motiv**, Motive	motive